Terror and Triumph

 **Marshall Cavendish** Benchmark

New York

Published by Marshall Cavendish Benchmark
An imprint of Marshall Cavendish Corporation

Website: www.marshallcavendish.us

This publication represents the opinions and views of the authors based on the authors' personal experience, knowledge, and research. The information in this book serves as a general guide only. The author and publisher have used their best efforts in preparing this book and disclaim liability rising directly and indirectly from the use and application of this book.

Other Marshall Cavendish Offices:
Marshall Cavendish International (Asia) Private Limited, 1 New Industrial Road, Singapore 536196 • Marshall Cavendish International (Thailand) Co Ltd. 253 Asoke, 12th Flr, Sukhumvit 21 Road, Klongtoey Nua, Wattana, Bangkok 10110, Thailand • Marshall Cavendish (Malaysia) Sdn Bhd, Times Subang, Lot 46, Subang Hi-Tech Industrial Park, Batu Tiga, 40000 Shah Alam, Selangor Darul Ehsan, Malaysia

Marshall Cavendish is a trademark of Times Publishing Limited

All websites were available and accurate when this book was sent to press.

Library of Congress Cataloging-in-Publication Data

Terror and triumph.
p. cm. -- (World War II)
Summary: "Covers the events of World War II including Operation Overlord, the Eastern European Front, the European Air War, and the Battle of the Atlantic"--Provided by publisher.
Includes bibliographical references and index.

ISBN 978-0-7614-4949-2
1. World War, 1939-1945--Campaigns--Juvenile literature. 2. World War, 1939-1945--Europe--Juvenile literature.

 D743.7.T47 2011
 940.54'21--dc22

2010012737

Senior Editor: Deborah Grahame-Smith
Publisher: Michelle Bisson
Art Director: Anahid Hamparian
Series Designer: Bill Smith Group

PICTURE CREDITS
Associated Press: 8, 38, 47, 62, 92, 109, (Henry L. Griffin) 114 (William C. Allen)
Getty Images: 22 (Cynthia Johnson/Time & Life Pictures)
Library of Congress: 14, 15, 16, 48, 57, 97, 98 (George Grantham Bain Collection), 122
Robert Hunt Library: 4, 34, 69, 70, 74, 89, 105, 110
United States Air Force: 86, 90, 93
United States Army: 32, 54, 114, 123
United States Naval Historical Center: 103
Shutterstock: 17 (Torsten Lorenz), 21 (Ivan Cholakov Gostock-dot-net), 25 (Olemac), 101 (Snaprender),

Additional imagery provided by U.S. Army, Joseph Gary Sheahan, 1944, Dreamstime.com, Shutterstock.com.

Printed in Malaysia (T)
135642

Contents

▶ The Irish Free State was officially neutral during the war. In this street scene from Dublin, the owners of the Swastika Laundry show their preference for Germany. Years of British colonialism perhaps prompted the laundry's decision to support the Nazis during the war.

1

The World and World War II, 1939 to 1945

KEY PEOPLE	KEY PLACES	
Adolf Hitler	Europe	India
Francisco Franco	British Commonwealth	Africa
	Latin America	Asia

One of the first casualties of World War II was neutrality. Certain European states, notably Ireland, Sweden, and Switzerland, were able to remain neutral throughout the war. Other countries, like Norway and Denmark, declared themselves neutral. But that did not keep them from being invaded.

Germany imported large quantities of iron ore from Sweden. In spring 1940 the British first lord of the admiralty, Winston Churchill, proposed mining Norwegian waters to prevent ships from carrying the iron to Germany. He also wanted to place British troops in Norway. He got his way. On April 5, troops landed at four Norwegian ports. Three days later minelayers entered Norwegian waters. But Britain's disregard for Norway's neutrality was a disaster. In June Norway succumbed to Nazi occupation. King Haakon VII and his ministers set up a government-in-exile in London.

In 1939 Denmark signed a treaty of nonaggression with Nazi Germany. Despite this, German forces overran the country in April 1940. The Danish monarch, Christian X, and his government were allowed to remain in place until 1943. All the same, the Danish minister in Washington, D.C., against instructions from the king, signed an agreement letting the United States set up military bases in Greenland. The Danish merchant marine served under Allied command, as did the Norwegian merchant marine.

The Irish Free State denied the British government the use of Irish ports.

The Irish Free State, or southern Ireland, was able to maintain its neutrality throughout the war. Less than twenty years earlier, it had cast off British rule. The Irish government protested against Allied military activity in Northern Ireland, which remained part of the United Kingdom. The Irish Free State denied the British government the use of Irish ports, which were badly needed in the Battle of the Atlantic.

German and Japanese agents enjoyed freedom of movement in Ireland throughout the war. The U.S. government asked Ireland to expel the Japanese and German ambassadors from Dublin in 1944. That request was turned down, and caused anger in the U.S. Nevertheless, a great number of Irish men volunteered for the British army. Even a German air raid on the capital, Dublin, on January 2, 1941, could not force Ireland to join the Allies. Some observers thought the raid was a warning of what would come if the Irish Free State were to give up its neutrality.

Spain was the great curiosity among the neutral nations. Its leader Francisco Franco kept Spain out of the war, even though the Germans and Italians had supported Franco in the Spanish Civil War. Franco also signed the Anti-Comintern Pact in 1939. While Franco himself was on the Axis side, he felt that Spain and his Fascist movement needed a period of peace and stability. After France fell in 1940, however, Franco announced that Spain was giving up neutrality for "nonbelligerency." That is, Spain would not fight, but it would help the Axis powers. Spain would provide German U-boats with harbors and refuelling stations, for example. The use of these ports let the submarines extend their range to the north coast of

FRANCISCO FRANCO

Francisco Franco (1892–1975) was the leader of the victorious nationalist side in the Spanish Civil War. He was the dictator of Spain from 1939 until his death in 1975. He liked to call himself the *caudillo*, which means "leader."

Franco spent his whole life in the army. He entered the officer corps in 1910 and was promoted to general in 1924. In the Moroccan colonial war, he developed the ruthlessness he later used to terrorize his opponents in Spain. When civil war broke out in 1936, Franco's goal was to "save Spain from Marxism at whatever cost." He quickly gained the military and political leadership of the nationalist cause. By the time the civil war ended in 1939, Spain lay at his mercy.

Franco began an "institutionalized revenge." He declared the nationalists had a list of 2 million Communists who should be punished. For years after, the Spanish newspapers printed long lists of executions, life imprisonment sentences, and exile to hard labor for anti-Fascist veterans of the civil war.

During World War II Hitler thought Franco was an evasive and exasperating ally. Franco signed the Anti-Comintern Pact, but he would not join the Tripartite Pact, which had been signed by Germany, Italy, and Japan in September 1940. Hitler tried to to persuade Franco to bring Spain into the war. Franco refused. In reply to the Führer's confidence in German victory, Franco asked troubling questions. After meeting with Franco for nine hours, Hitler told Mussolini that "rather than go through that again he [Hitler] would prefer to have three or four teeth taken out."

Brazil. Spain also sent supplies to German garrisons on the Atlantic coast. In October 1940 Hitler visited Franco in southern France. But he could not convince the Spanish dictator to join the Axis. Spain remained on the sidelines until the end.

Two other major European nations stayed neutral throughout World War II: Switzerland and Sweden. Switzerland was never really a target for German invasion. Its value to Hitler was that it was a good place to do business. The Swiss franc was the only truly convertible currency used worldwide throughout the war. Germany used Swiss banks to exchange looted gold for Swiss francs. The Swiss currency was then used to pay for war supplies.

Sweden, although officially neutral, allowed German troops to be transported across Swedish territory when Germany occupied Norway and Denmark in 1940. However, Sweden withdrew this support in 1943 when it became clear that Germany would lose the war.

The changing fortunes of Nazi Germany also played a role in Turkey's policies. A 1939 alliance with Britain and France died when it seemed like Germany's Blitzkrieg victories would bring Allied defeat. After the Axis invasion of the Soviet Union in June 1941, Turkey signed a nonaggression pact with Germany. Still, Turkey's president, Ismet Inönö, managed to preserve neutrality until February 1945. But when Allied victory was on the horizon, he sided with the Allies.

German Chancellor Adolf Hitler (left) and Generalissimo Francisco Franco (right) salute to the crowds in a ceremony during Hitler's visit to France, Spain, and Italy in October 1940.

Latin America and the War

By the start of World War II, most Latin American countries had been independent of European colonial rule since the early nineteenth century. Rule by dictators or by the military was common. In 1939, governments throughout the continent largely supported the Axis powers.

Such support for Axis powers was, therefore, not surprising because Latin Americans had few good reasons to side with the Allies. The United States and Britain had exploited Latin American resources and intervened in their affairs. For example, historical events in Argentina did not lead its people to prefer parliamentary institutions to authoritarian rule. Likewise, almost every major Latin American country in 1939 expressed some support for Germany.

The notable exception was Mexico. Its location in North America with its economic ties with the U.S. drew Mexico to the Allied side. Mexico and Brazil were the only Latin American countries to play an active part in the war, both on the Allied side. At their peak, the Brazilian armed forces in World War II numbered 200,000. Their losses amounted to 1,000 killed or missing and 4,000 wounded. A quarter of a million Mexicans living in the United States served in the U.S. armed forces. Mexico also supplied labor for U.S. agriculture in the southern states and produced minerals for the United States' defense industry.

Mexico and Brazil were the only Latin American countries to play an active part in the war, both on the Allied side.

Among the pro-Axis Latin American countries, pro-German feeling was strongest in Argentina, including solid popular support for the Nazis. Argentina had a large German population and an even greater Italian one. The wealthy Spaniards who dominated Argentina's economic and political life supported Franco. Chile was also strongly pro-Axis, largely out of fear of an Axis victory and the desire to be on the winning side. When the war began, the president of Chile was Pedro Aguirre Cerda. Elected in 1938 as a Popular Front candidate, Cerda had support from both the Communists and Chile's Nazis.

The Soviet-German nonaggression pact of 1939 kept Chile distant from the Allied powers. Chile's long coastline made its people fearful. In both Chile and Argentina there was suppression of pro-Allied opinions and support. There was also anger at the United States' undersecretary of state for Latin American affairs, Sumner Welles. He denounced pro-Axis activities in those countries. This was seen as intervention in the internal politics of sovereign nations.

Latin America and the United States

By 1942 the Axis cause was not as popular in Latin America, partly because of pressure exerted by the United States. In 1910 a permanent Pan-American Union, based in Washington, D.C., had been created. The Union had achieved little, since most Latin American states resented the leadership and dominance of the United States. But in a 1933 conference the U. S. agreed to the principle of nonintervention in the affairs of other nations in the western hemisphere. That step helped foster cooperation at a 1938 conference at Lima, Peru. There, it was agreed to respond as one to any threat of foreign intervention. Those advances in U.S.–Latin American relations were part of Franklin Roosevelt's "Good Neighbor" policy.

After the Japanese attack on Pearl Harbor in December 1941, another international conference was held at Rio de Janeiro, Brazil. The United States wanted the conference to give unanimous support to the Allied powers. Nine countries (eight of them from Central America and the Caribbean) had already broken diplomatic relations with Germany and her allies. At the 1942 conference, every Latin American country did so except Chile and Argentina. In May 1942 Mexico entered the war on the Allied side. Brazil followed in August.

Early in 1943 Chile broke with the Axis, and Argentina did so in January 1944. What changed their minds was the fear of American reprisals and the lure of American investment in their industries. Since turning their backs on Germany and Japan, Peru and Paraguay had received much-needed American financial aid. Argentina in particular wanted similar help.

Juan Perón (1895–1974) was an officer in the Argentinian army. He became popular after he helped engineer the overthrow the government of Ramón Castillo in 1943. He was a leader of army officers who were inspired by Italian Fascism and German national socialism. The officers wanted to make Argentina the major power in South America.

In the new military government, Perón served as secretary of labor and social welfare. Then he became minister of war, and finally vice-president. He was the real power behind Edelmiro Farrell's government. Perón backed the trade unions. He brought in radical welfare reform. He raised wages and provided paid holidays. The popular support he gained from workers was the foundation of his power.

Perón's political doctrine was called *Justicialismo*. In it, Facism and socialism mixed together. He aimed for national unity and an end to class divisions. He did not challenge the basic social structure or the inequalities in Argentinian life. Perón's political approach gained him the support of everyday workers in the labor force, the Catholic Church, and the conservative Fascist elements within the society.

Senior army officers became alarmed at this popularity. Perón was briefly imprisoned in 1945, after a coup. Mariá Eva Duarte, a radio actress and singer known as Evita, organized mass pro-Perón marches of the *descamisados* (or the "shirtless ones"). The descamisados were members of trade unions that Perón later turned into the quasi-military wing of his political party.

When Perón was released from prison, he married Evita. She had charismatic appeal to the poor of Argentina, because she had been born into poverty. Perón was elected president of Argentina in 1946. Within a few years, he established a dictatorship in Argentina, which became a haven for ex-Nazis after the war.

When Perón was overthrown in 1955, he went into exile. He was allowed to return in 1973, and was once more elected president. After only nine months in office, he died in 1974.

Most Latin American nations enjoyed prosperity during the war, thanks to increased exports at high prices. The countries also realized how dependent their economies were on the United States and Britain. Such dependence was resented. The experience of world war twice in the same century sharpened the desire of Latin Americans for real independence from foreign control. However, their experience in World War II showed most of all that, despite some regimes with pro-Nazi leanings, the people of Latin America wanted to align themselves solidly with the Western world.

India and the War

In September 1939 it was not clear that the war in Europe would greatly affect India, even though India was the largest country in the British Empire. Indian opinion, though against Nazism, was clouded by anticolonial ideals that made it hard to rally to Britain's side.

In 1914, at the outbreak of World War I, Britain committed India to a "war for freedom." But the promised freedom was withheld. Indians thought that the new world war was none of their business. A continued difficulty for most Indians was that Britain postponed discussion of independent Dominion status. This status meant some autonomy for India until "after the war." So, Indians were happy to accept the opinion of military experts that the war was to be a mechanized one. As a result, the unmechanized Indian army had no part to play in it.

The Indian army distinguished itself in many campaigns. In particular, Indian Divisions were seen as among the best troops mustered by the Allies.

The outlook changed with the spread of fighting to the Middle East and with Japan's entry into the war in 1941. By the beginning of 1942 India was a supply center for the Middle East and the home of South East Asia Command. The Indian army distinguished itself in many campaigns. In particular, Indian Divisions were seen as among the best troops mustered by the Allies.

India's participation in the war forced the British government to make a new political promise. When war broke out, Indians were greatly offended when the viceroy, the British monarch's representative, announced that since Britain was at war, so was India. In February 1940 the Indian National Congress denounced the British government for declaring India to be belligerent, and for exploiting Indian resources in the war effort. Nothing short of independence from Britain would do, the Congress asserted. In 1942 new proposals from the British still had a feeling of "after the war" about them. The Congress rejected them. Negotiations continued as the Japanese occupied Burma and the Japanese navy lurked in the Bay of Bengal. Gandhi argued that any continuation of British rule in India could provoke the Japanese.

The Congress ordered Britain out of India, with what became known as the "Quit India" resolution. In response, the British Raj (the British authorities in India), outlawed the Congress Party and imprisoned its leaders, Gandhi and Jawaharlal Nehru, along with some 60,000 other nationalists. Even after that, 3 million Indian volunteers joined the British army. Churchill, always opposed to Indian independence, was impressed. But it was the Raj's last display of real authority. After the war in 1947 the Indian people, partitioned into India and Pakistan, at last threw off British imperialism.

The British Dominions and the War

The self-governing Dominions of the British Commonwealth and Empire, namely Canada, Australia, New Zealand, and South Africa, needed to decide their own foreign and defense policy, in the light of their national interests, during the war. In 1937 the Canadian prime minister, Mackenzie King, publicly stated his doubt that any British Dominion would again send an expeditionary force to Europe. At the same time, New Zealand and Australia expressed an interest in formulating a united Commonwealth foreign policy. Canada refused to commit itself to support whatever foreign actions the British government might take. In South Africa, scarred by memories of the war between the British and the Dutch Boers at the beginning of the twentieth century, opinion was divided. The racist and largely Boer Nationalist Party was firmly in the Axis camp. It hoped an Axis victory would lead to South Africa's becoming a republic. Afrikaners (as the Dutch settlers were known), although not all pro-Axis, were nevertheless not willing to side with Britain. They argued for some sort of neutrality.

The majority of white South Africans disagreed, however, with the neutralist stance of the government of General Barry Hertzog. As a result, his government was voted out of office. A new government, headed by Jan Christian Smuts, declared war on Germany on September 6, 1939.

Smuts was determined to back the Allies. He was certain that the Nazi threat to freedom had to be met. Smuts felt that South Africa's future lay within the British Commonwealth. South Africa's industry and agriculture were geared to support the Allied war effort.

The country's armed forces—two full-strength active service divisions, an air force, and ships for coastal defense—played a larger role than they had played in World War I. South African forces fought in British units all over the world, distinguishing themselves in the Allied liberation of Abyssinia (Ethiopia), North Africa, Madagascar, and Italy.

Smuts [head of South Africa] was determined to back the Allies.

These Australian troops saw service against Japanese forces on Buna in New Guinea. The command leader has jumped on the tank to warn the men inside of a Japanese pillbox (concrete fortification for a sniper) that he has spotted enemy forces on the trail.

All of the British Dominions did eventually support liberal democracy in Europe. Australia and New Zealand did so without hesitation, believing that if Britain was at war, so were they. Canadians had moved further away from ties to the crown. As late as March 1939, when Hitler seized what was left of Czechoslovakia, the Canadian prime minister was still neutral. He declared in parliament: "The idea that every twenty years this country should automatically and as a matter of course take part in a war overseas for democracy or self-determination of other small nations, that a country which has all it can do to run itself should feel called upon to save, periodically, a continent that cannot save itself . . . seems to many a nightmare and sheer madness." Along with Canada, North American isolationist yearnings were not confined to the United States.

However, unlike the United States, Canada entered the war against Germany on September, 10, 1939. Canada became a major supply base for Britain in the difficult months before the Lend-Lease agreement between the United States and Britain came into effect. One million Canadians served in the army overseas, and the Royal Canadian Navy, which expanded greatly during the war years, played a major convoy role in the Atlantic and in the Normandy landings in 1944.

Nationalism in Africa and Asia

European colonies experienced contrasting fortunes in World War II. Some Asian dependencies like French Indochina, Dutch Indonesia, and British Malaya, fell into enemy hands. Most of the African colonies, on the other hand, found themselves valued as assets in the war against the Axis powers. They were valued not only for military personnel, but for the products of their mines and plantations. In either case, the war helped introduce the era of decolonization. This process would continue to be prominent in world politics between 1945 and 1965. World War II shook the power of the imperial rulers. So the effort that the colonies put into the war made it impossible to imagine that in peacetime the old subservience of "subject races" to

In either case, the war helped introduce the era of decolonization.

their masters could go on. The very idea that the world could be classified into "advanced" and "backward" nations was becoming outdated.

In 1944 there were two different expressions of how acceptable anti-imperialism had become: the Brazzaville Conference in January and the "Philadelphia Charter" issued in May. At Brazzaville in Central Africa, Free France, the anti-Nazi resistance movement, held a conference on the future of France's colonies. Presiding over the conference was the movement's leading figure, General Charles de Gaulle. With an inability to feel which way the wind was starting to blow, the conference ruled out independence. Instead, they called for the development of local assemblies to express colonial opinion.

Additionally, colonial representatives would be able to sit in the French national assembly. In May 1946 the French assembly proclaimed that "all subjects of overseas territories [now] possess the same rights as French

General Charles de Gaulle of France presided over the conference at Brazzaville in Central Africa in 1944.

citizens in the home country." The French government ignored the growing demands for independence coming from colonies such as Algeria and Indochina. But the proclamation helped to set the tone for postwar anticolonial movements that gathered increasing momentum.

The Philadelphia Charter, which resulted from a meeting of forty-one member nations of the International Labor Organization, proclaimed the right of all human beings "to pursue both their material well-being and their spiritual development in conditions of freedom and dignity." It also stated that "the attainment of the conditions in which this shall be possible must constitute the central aim of national and international policy." Such a proclamation was ambitious. But the war would help bring an end to colonial rule everywhere in the world, in Southeast Asia and Indonesia, in Africa, and in the Middle East states "mandated" to France and Britain.

Spies and Spying

The use of spies is not always the best way to gain information about the enemy. In World War II spying took second place to intelligence from radio interception and code breaking. Human espionage played its part, although both the Germans and the Allies were better at infiltrating the enemy's spy rings than at spying themselves. Almost all the German spies

Spying on citizens was commonplace in Nazi Germany. The Nazi seal on this envelope means that it has been opened and its contents examined for unexplained reasons.

LEOPOLD TREPPER

Leopold Trepper (1904–1982), code-named "Otto," was a Polish Jew. He was head of the Soviet spy network called the Red Orchestra. During the war he spent most of his time in Paris, where he was known as Jean Gilbert, a "Belgian industrialist." He and fellow agents Leo Grossvogel and Hillel Katz worked for a fictional company, "Simex." In his memoirs he gave a detailed account of his spying.

Twice a week I went to one of the twenty to twenty-five hideouts Leo had selected—usually a villa in the suburbs. Katz or Grossvogel, who had gathered intelligence, would bring me this material. I sorted it and classified it; from this mass of information I wrote a brief, condensed report. A liaison agent then took charge of the material and passed it on to a coder. Each stage of the process was carefully separated from the others. The members of the network knew only what was absolutely indispensable. From the beginning we paid particular attention to the technique of the rendezvous.

Two agents who were to meet would leave their homes well before the hour set for the rendezvous. As a rule, they would take the Metro, always riding in the last car and getting off among the last to leave so that they could watch the other passengers. Then they would transfer to another line and repeat the same procedure until they were absolutely certain they were not being followed. Each of the two liaison agents would then go into a telephone booth agreed on in advance and look in the phone book to see whether the code word had been underlined—for example, the tenth name in the second column of a particular page—which would indicate that the coast was clear. The meeting itself, which had to look accidental, never lasted more than a few seconds and usually took place in the corridors of the Metro.

The dispatches were discreetly passed from hand to hand. In the case of very important information, we used invisible ink and wrote between the lines of a perfectly innocuous letter. We made it a rule never to say anything over the telephone.

Taken from Trepper's *The Great Game* (London: Michael Joseph, 1977).

sent to the United States and Canada were uncovered, usually by intercepting radio transmissions. In addition, the best intelligence was not always gathered by professional agents. Spies came in all shapes and sizes. A Belgian railway clerk, for example, provided the Allies with daily lists of German war materials that passed through his station.

Among professional agents none, perhaps, was more famous than Richard Sorge, a German convert to Communism. He was based in Tokyo as a foreign correspondent for Dutch and German newspapers and was employed by the Soviet Union as a spy. His job as press attaché to the German embassy in Tokyo gave him access to high-level officials. He learned of the Nazis' plan to invade the USSR in May 1941, and passed the information on to the Russian government in Moscow. Sorge's information was discredited by his superiors. The invasion, when it came, was a shock. He was also able to relate to his superiors the news that Japan was not planning to attack the USSR. As a result, Soviet troops were instead used to fight the Battle of Moscow in late 1941. Sorge was eventually betrayed and was executed in 1944.

The Soviet Union played a double role during the war. Suspicious of the capitalist West, and aware that the alliance with Washington, D.C. and London would collapse once the war was over, Stalin had scores of agents against these wartime allies. The most notorious of them was a group of Englishmen, all graduates of Cambridge University—Kim Philby, Donald Maclean, Guy Burgess, John Cairncross, and Anthony Blunt—who became known as "The Five." They infiltrated the highest reaches of British civil service and the intelligence service itself. The usefulness of their information remains in doubt, since Stalin was actually more interested in events that never came about—a German peace and a British invasion of the USSR.

No Allied spy had more direct influence on any military campaign than Rygor Slowikowski, a Polish refugee whose business was making cereals in Algiers, Morocco. He was head of the spy ring known as Agency Africa. The success of the Allied campaign to conquer North Africa at the end of 1942 depended heavily on information passed on by Slowikowski to the U.S. intelligence department, the Office of Strategic Services (OSS).

> *No Allied spy had more direct influence on a military campaign than Rygor Slowikowski, a Polish refugee whose business was making cereals in Algiers, Morocco.*

Allied Economic Warfare

Twice in modern European history one man has attempted to lead his country, by force of arms, to dominate the continent. On each occasion, against Napoleon and against Hitler, the effort to block that ambition included economic warfare. In each case Britain tried to use its command of the seas to stop the import of vital goods by the enemy. A Ministry of Economic Warfare was set up in Britain as soon as war broke out in September 1939. The American equivalent was the Board of Economic Warfare, established in 1941. Curiously, although the Germans attacked Allied merchant shipping on the high seas and for a brief period during the Blitz bombed England's western ports, economic warfare never figured highly in German military thinking.

A naval blockade was key to the Allies' economic warfare against the Axis.

A naval blockade was key to the Allies' economic warfare against the Axis. After Pearl Harbor, the British effort to stop goods from entering Germany was joined by the American attempt to embargo trade with Japan. The most important objective of the blockades was to restrict the flow of raw materials essential for arms production. One method was novel: the United States and its allies, for example, sought to buy up certain scarce items, crucial to the Axis war effort, simply to keep them from the enemy.

Economic blockade was of little effect in Europe once Germany occupied most of the continent and Italy had come in on the Axis side. For the first two years of the war, the Soviet–German nonaggression pact also ensured a flow of essential food and materials into Germany from the USSR.

The Soviet Union also provided a land link between Japan and Germany. Japan was heavily dependent on the import of raw materials and by 1944 began to show clear signs of suffering from the lack of them. Economic blockades had less of an impact on German arms production. Even at the end of 1944, when the situation was darkest for the Nazi regime, German industrial production, of steel and coal especially, continued to expand. However, in one important aspect the Allies were successful. They kept oil and fuel from reaching Germany, weakening the Luftwaffe.

After D-Day in 1944, Allied forces dropped one megaton of bombs on German industry.

Important as the blockades were, in World War II air bombardment mattered just as much. From 1943 onward the destruction of industries was a central goal of the Allied bombing of Germany. The last bombing offensive against Germany began in the late spring of 1944 and increased so much that over half the bombs—just over one megaton in total—that fell on Germany were dropped after D-Day on June 6, 1944. An attack of that magnitude was bound to show results. German war production did decline, though never so far as to pre-1942 levels. The German economy did suffer from that one-megaton attack, but historians have questioned whether the resources devoted to bombing might have been better spent on defeating the German army.

▶The Allied Invasion of Normandy, code-named Operation Overlord, on D-Day was the largest amphibious assault in history. The success or failure of the D-Day invasion on June 6, 1944, would determine the outcome of the war.

2 Operation Overlord

KEY PEOPLE	KEY PLACES	
Omar Bradley	**CITIES**	**REGIONS**
Dwight D. Eisenhower	Caen, France	Normandy, France
Bernard Montgomery	Cherbourg, France	Pas-de-Calais, France
Erwin Rommel	Dieppe, France	

On June 6, 1944, or D-Day, the western Allies launched Operation Overlord, the largest amphibious attack in history. The attack targeted five beaches of Normandy, France. Their code names were Utah, Omaha, Gold, Juno, and Sword. This attack would force Hitler to fight a war on two fronts—a war he could not win.

The previous night, the British Broadcasting Corporation (BBC) had played a seemingly random line of French poetry. German listening stations picked up the phrase, but dismissed it. This phrase was a code. It informed the French Resistance that the Allies would invade within forty-eight hours. The French Resistance began to sabotage German communications and transportation targets. These raids—about 1,000 of them—confused the Germans and made it hard for them to move troops into Normandy over the next few days.

Planning the Invasion

The D-Day invasion had taken years of careful planning. These plans had included many delays, diversions, and disagreements. The British and Americans had hammered out their disagreements at a series of conferences. The United States had entered the war in December 1941, after the Japanese attack on Pearl Harbor. At that time, nearly 75 percent of Germany's armed forces were pitted against the Soviets. Joseph Stalin demanded that Great Britain and the United States invade German-held Europe. This invasion would be a second front, and would take pressure off the Soviets.

American and British political leaders met in late 1941 and early 1942. They agreed on a strategy of "Germany First." However, they had trouble agreeing on either a date or a location for the opening of the second front.

The U. S. wanted to destroy Germany quickly so that they could turn their attention to fighting Japan.

The U. S. wanted to destroy Germany quickly so that they could turn their attention to fighting Japan. They called for an invasion of France within a year.

The British felt that there were not enough resources for a full-scale landing in Europe during 1942. They convinced the Americans to send troops to fight in North Africa instead. The North Africa campaign further delayed the invasion of France. However, the Allies did agree on a rehearsal for the future landings. This decision led to the raid on the city of Dieppe, France, in August. This raid was a test of how easy it would be to capture a German-held port.

The Dieppe landing was a disaster. But, the Allies learned valuable lessons that helped the D-Day landings in June 1944 to succeed.

In early 1943 the British convinced the Americans to finish the campaign in North Africa and then invade Sicily and mainland Italy. However, the British did finally agree to an invasion of France. But the invasion would require thousands of landing boats, called amphibious assault craft. These boats were not yet built. It would take until 1944 at the earliest to build the boats.

PLANNING D-DAY

The Allied D-Day planners had a gigantic task. They had to find some suitable site for invasion and confuse the Germans as to their intentions. They also had to organize an assault plan involving vast air, land, and sea forces.

The first job was to choose a section of the long German-occupied coast of western Europe, Hitler's Atlantic Wall, which would be best for invasion. The planners considered the winds, tides, and terrain of the area and the strength of the local defenses. They eliminated places that were beyond the range of fighter planes based in England.

The Allies concentrated on northern France. They rejected the area of France closest to England, the region called the Pas-de-Calais, because of the steep cliffs along the shore. The Normandy region was 80 miles (130 km) farther away than Calais, but it had wide beaches. A major port, Cherbourg, was nearby. By June 1943 the choice was clear: Normandy would be the target for D-Day.

Deception and Spying

The Germans suspected that the Allies would invade, but the D-Day planners misled them. Hitler unintentionally helped. He thought the allies would land in the Pas-de-Calais region. He ordered many of his available forces to strengthen the Pas-de-Calais, instead of other sectors of his Atlantic Wall.

The Allies used tricks to confirm Hitler's belief. They transmitted fake radio messages and spread false rumors. They constructed dummy dockyards, equipment, and camps in southeast England, the region nearest the Pas-de-Calais. They used radio traffic to create two fictitious armies, one in the southeast and the other in Scotland to suggest an invasion of Norway. The Germans never suspected that they were being deceived. At the same time, Allied agents, helped by the French Resistance, were gathering information about German defenses in Normandy.

Planning the Landings

D-Day itself included several interconnected operations. First, the naval operation included transporting the troops across the English Channel and bombarding the German defenses. Then ships and landing boats would have to get the troops and equipment ashore. In total, the Allies used 6,939 vessels, including 1,213 warships and 4,126 landing craft.

Second, the air effort had several phases. Starting in April, bombers attacked communications and radar sites to isolate Normandy from reinforcements. On D-Day bombing raids attacked the German beach defenses. Also, thousands of troops landed by parachute and glider near the beaches. Finally, fighter planes flew to provide cover against any German counterattacks. On D-Day the Allies deployed 4,400 bombers, 3,800 fighters, 1,350 transports, 3,500 gliders, and 500 reconnaissance aircraft.

Third, the landings themselves took place. The top priority was to land the successive waves of troops and equipment at the right time and place. The troops would then have to fight their way inland as quickly as possible.

At the Trident Conference in May 1943 the Allies agreed to an invasion date of May 1, 1944. A group of American and British officers were given the job of planning the invasion. In December American General Dwight D. Eisenhower was named supreme Allied commander and placed in command of the operation: SHAEF (Supreme Headquarters Allied Expeditionary Force). However, Eisenhower soon had to give up on the planned May 1 date because there were not enough landing boats. The invasion date was pushed back to early June 1944.

Buildup to D-Day: Operation Bolero

Two years earlier, in January 1942, the United States began to build up troops and equipment in Great Britain, to prepare for an invasion of Europe. The buildup was code-named Bolero.

The flow across the Atlantic started as a trickle. At first, in the wake of the attack on Pearl Harbor, the United States was concentrating on defending its own coastline and its Pacific bases against the Japanese. Few forces were available to fulfill all these roles. The U.S. military had to expand quickly to train and equip millions of recruits.

By mid-1944, 1.5 million American personnel were stationed in Britain.

More and more troops began to arrive in Great Britain after mid-1943. The U.S. Army was swelling with new troops, and the Japanese had been halted in the Pacific. By mid-1944, 1.5 million American personnel were stationed in Britain. They lived in huge, tented camps and spent their time in a seemingly endless round of training focused on amphibious assault techniques.

The Question of Weather

By late May 1944 Eisenhower knew that he would soon have to make the decision to begin the invasion. The troops were now trained and battle-ready. The biggest obstacle now was the weather. Only three days of each month had just the right combination of tide and time they needed to land in Normandy. During that time, skies would have to be at least partly clear so that aircraft could bomb accurately. The small landing craft could not sail in rough seas.

WHERE WILL THE ALLIES INVADE?

On D-Day, the British and Americans had to move vast numbers of warships across the English Channel, then land the assault troops in the right place at the right time.

First, Allied destroyers and antisubmarine aircraft sealed off the channel from possible German counterattacks. Allied fighters roared overhead, while warships patrolled alongside the invasion fleet.

The invasion force, a total of some 285,000 troops, had assembled at ports along the English coast. They set sail at different times because of the varied distances they had to travel. All these ships came together at a position, code-named Z, in the central channel. They then sailed directly south toward Normandy.

About 12 miles (19 km) off the French coast the huge fleet split into two groups. The Western Task Force headed toward Omaha and Utah beaches. The Eastern Task Force sailed toward Gold, Juno, and Sword beaches. Warships began to fire their heavy guns at enemy positions. Five groups of assault craft formed up for the final run in to the beaches. The whole transportation operation went according to the Allied plan, giving D-Day the best possible start.

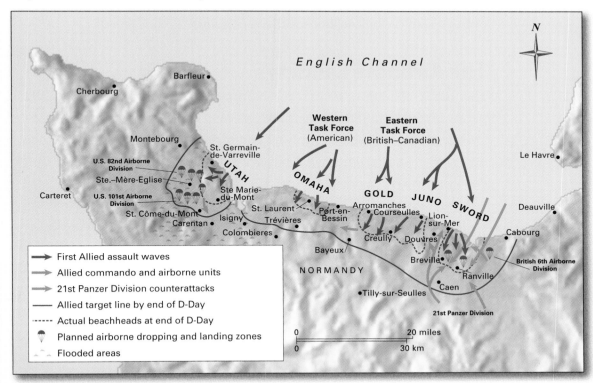

The Allies selected five beaches for Operation Overlord, the Allied Invasion of France on June 6, 1944.

On May 29, weather experts predicted acceptable weather in the days ahead. The order was given to begin the complex process of loading troops and equipment onto their ships. But on June 3, with the men and equipment mostly loaded, the weather began to worsen.

Eisenhower's chief meteorologist, Group Captain James Stagg, predicted that violent storms would cross southern Britain on June 4. Eisenhower ordered a twenty-four-hour delay. Then Stagg predicted that the weather would be calmer for twenty-four hours, starting on the afternoon of June 5. This was an uncomfortably small opening. It might permit the arrival of the initial landing force in Normandy. But if storms returned, the follow-up waves of troops would not be able to land. Eisenhower consulted his senior generals, including Britain's Field Marshal Bernard Montgomery. But Eisenhower himself made the final decision on the morning of June 5. Stagg stuck to his belief that the weather would briefly improve. Eisenhower made up his mind: "OK, we'll go." At these brief words, 5,000 Allied ships put to sea from the coast of southern England.

The Airborne Landings

The first Allied forces to arrive in Normandy were 24,000 British and U.S. paratroopers who landed near the invasion beaches in the early hours of D-Day. Their job was to hold back any major German response in the first hours of the main landings. They would hold key positions until troops from the beaches reached them.

The British paratroopers achieved most of their objectives by daybreak.

Stationed near the Anglo-Canadian landing beaches at Caen was a German panzer division. To block a German counterattack, 200 glider-borne British paratroopers swooped down on two bridges over the Orne River and Caen Canal shortly after midnight. Taking the Germans by surprise, they captured the bridges in minutes. Other troops landed soon after, by parachute and glider. They captured heavy German guns, key river bridges, and various pieces of high ground. The British paratroopers achieved most of their objectives by daybreak. To the west, U.S. airborne troops landed at 1:30 a.m. to capture bridges and key positions near Utah Beach. However, transport aircraft veered off targets due to poor navigation, low clouds, and enemy fire. Most paratroopers missed their drop zones. Some troops landed in the water of flooded fields and drowned. Others were lost in the darkness and confused, attacking anything.

The Germans were also confused. The U. S. paratroopers managed to capture some bridges and destroy others, as well as one key village, Ste.-Mère-Eglise. Not able to achieve all their objectives, the landings had helped to protect the main D-Day invasion on the beaches.

KEY FIGURES

DWIGHT D. EISENHOWER

General Dwight D. Eisenhower (1890–1969) led the Allied forces in western Europe from late 1943 until the end of the war. He was an outstanding leader and strategist. He was also very good at soothing the tensions that threatened to break up the U.S.-British alliance.

Eisenhower was chosen as supreme Allied commander in December 1943. The British had wanted one of their own generals to lead the invasion of France. However, Roosevelt fought for Eisenhower's selection. The British finally agreed, partly because Eisenhower had shown his skills as a planner and leader during the fighting in North Africa, Sicily, and Italy.

Eisenhower had great military skill and experience. He was also very likeable. He often managed to calmly settle disagreements between his British and U.S. generals. Later, his charm and war record enabled him to win two terms as U.S. president.

General Dwight D. Eisenhower

The American Sector: Pre-dawn Preparation

At 3:00 a.m. on D-Day the 1,000 warships of the Western Task Force took up positions 12 miles (19 km) off Omaha and Utah beaches. The first waves of invasion troops began to climb down from their large transport ships to the smaller landing craft. Strong winds had whipped up the English Channel. The landing craft bucked and rolled in the darkness. The troops, nervous and seasick, settled into their boats. They began the three-and-a-half-hour run in to shore.

Dawn came some two hours later. The Allied warships began a ferocious bombardment of the German shore defenses. More than 600 bombers flew in to drop their loads of bombs. The sight of the blasts and smoke comforted the assault troops. An observer heard one nervous GI exclaim: "Look what they're doing to those Germans. I guess there won't be a man alive there." In reality, the guns and bombs were doing very little damage. The defenders were protected by concrete-and-steel bunkers. Only a direct hit would kill them or knock out their weapons.

The landings were scheduled to begin at 6:30 a.m., the time of the lowest tide. One reason for this was to let the crews of the boats see the obstacles that were designed to rip the bottoms out of their vessels or blow them out of the water. These obstacles would be hidden underwater at high tide. The other reason was to give the invading troops the maximum amount of room on the beach on which to land and spread out. If there were any long delay, the tide would begin to come in. The higher tide would make the beaches narrower and narrower, forcing Allied troops to bunch up. As the troops gathered, they would become easy targets for the Germans.

It was vital that the first troops ashore make their way inland quickly to make room on the beaches. . . .There would be no place to hide from German gunfire.

It was vital that the first troops ashore make their way inland quickly to make room for those following. The first troops arriving at low tide would have to cross wide, flat beaches. There would be no place to hide from German gunfire. The troops would also risk heavy losses.

Utah Beach: First Landing

The first beach landings of D-Day took place on the westernmost beach, code-named Utah. The very first troops to come ashore were demolition teams. Their job was to clear explosive mines and other beach obstacles. This activity would open the path for the assault waves that followed. When their landing craft reached a point some 300 yards (100 m) out, the gunfire from the warships stopped. To avoid hitting Allied troops, the ships shifted their aim to targets farther inland. The 300 men of the first wave landed just one minute behind schedule. As the boats' bow ramps dropped, the men expected to run into a hail of enemy fire. Instead, the beach was eerily quiet, with only the sound of scattered fire. The men jumped down from their landing vehicles into the knee-deep water to wade some 100 yards (30 m) or so to dry land.

Americans suffered fewer than 200 casualties. The Utah Beach landing had been a major success.

In fact, Utah was comparatively lightly defended. The Germans considered it an unlikely target for an invasion. Also, many defenders in this area had been killed, wounded, or disoriented by the bombardment. The American troops had a key weapon on their side: amphibious tanks. These were special Sherman tanks. They had canvas flotation screens that let them float like boats. They had propellers that moved them slowly forward in water. Approximately thirty amphibious Sherman tanks soon came ashore. The Shermans' cannons and machine guns gave the ground troops valuable support.

The Germans had one major strongpoint in this area. This position was quickly captured. The capture opened up a road leading inland from the beach. American troops were able to push 5 miles (8 km) inland by nightfall, linking up with some of the scattered paratroopers who had dropped in before dawn. Most importantly, their actions created a path off the beach for the thousands troops and vehicles that were still landing. Because of their efforts, the Americans suffered fewer than 200 casualties. The Utah Beach landing was a major success.

Bloody Omaha: The Fighting Escalates

While the Utah landings were going well, events at Omaha Beach took a much deadlier turn. For hours, it seemed that the operation at Omaha Beach might crumble into disaster. If it had failed, the entire Allied invasion might have been doomed.

The Allied leaders knew that Omaha Beach would be difficult. The shape of the land itself was a problem. The beach was hemmed in by a salt marsh and cliffs. There were only a few possible ways for men and vehicles to move off the beaches. German defenses were strong in this area. The defenders could rake the beaches with fire. Also, a new German unit had recently arrived in this area. They were the 352nd Infantry Division, skilled veterans of the eastern front.

Allied planners hoped that the bombs and naval gunfire would knock out most of the German positions. They also sent one of the U.S. Army's best units, the 1st Infantry Division. These troops had proven themselves in combat in North Africa and Sicily. Finally, about sixty amphibious Sherman tanks were sent to Omaha Beach.

The Omaha operation went badly. The bombers and naval fire had mostly missed their targets. The seas were even rougher than at Utah, and several landing craft sank. The waves were also too high for the amphibious Shermans. Many sank in deep water.

The first wave of troops landed around 6:36 a.m. About half of them were instantly cut down by German fire. These first troops were supposed to clear paths through the beach obstacles for the follow-up waves of landing craft. Instead, the men were pinned down by enemy machine guns. This meant that landing craft ran into the beach obstacles and sank; others landed at the wrong place. As more troops arrived, some had to leave their boats in deeper waters. Weighed down by their gear, many drowned. Without the tanks to provide support, the Americans could do little against the dug-in Germans.

EYEWITNESS

HARRY PARLEY

Harry Parley was a young American soldier who came ashore on Omaha Beach. He described the scene this way.

Along the beach I could see burning wreckage and equipment, damaged landing craft and, of course, men trying to get off the beach. I realized that we had landed in the wrong beach sector and that many of the people around me were from other units and were strangers to me. What's more the terrain before us was not what I had been trained to encounter. All disorganized, all trying to stay alive, I remember removing my flamethrower and trying to dig a trench while lying on my stomach. Scared, worried, and often praying, I tried to help some of the wounded. One or two times I was able to control my fear long enough to race across the sand to drag a helpless GI out of the water and save him from drowning in the incoming tide. That was the extent of my bravery that morning.

Extract taken from Russell Miller's *Nothing Less Than Victory: The Oral History of D-Day*, 1993.

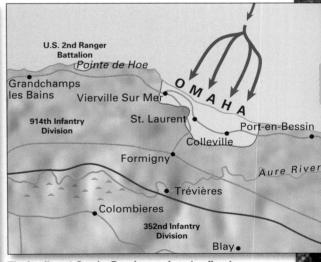

The landing at Omaha Beach was almost a disaster.

ALLIED SPECIALIZED EQUIPMENT

A Sherman tank clears mines preparing the beaches of Normandy for invasion.

Landing and Supply Craft Assault ships came in a range of sizes and types. The large Landing Craft Tank (LCT) was an ocean-going vessel that could carry sixty tanks. The much smaller Landing Craft Assault (LCA) carried about forty troops. The LCA would be shipped on a larger vessel and placed in the water near the objective.

Another type of boat, the Landing Craft Tank (Rocket), could launch 1,080 small rockets in thirty seconds. There was also the DUKW (Duck), which looked like a boat with wheels. It was highly useful for moving supplies from sea to land.

The Funnies The British led the development of specialized tanks for D-Day. They build several types, called "Funnies" by the troops. Some tanks were fitted with rotating drums and chains. These could blast paths through minefields. Another kind of tank fired a high-explosive shell the size of a trash can. These could destroy concrete bunkers. The most common type of special tank was the amphibious Sherman tank. It could sail ashore under its own power—at least in calm seas.

Supply The Allies built two giant artificial harbors known as Mulberries. These were made up of huge concrete structures and deliberately sunken ships. Put together, they formed floating roadways that let cargo ships unload trucks, which could drive directly to the shore. The Allies also built a system of flexible fuel pipes called PLUTO (Pipeline Under The Ocean). Laid on the bottom of the English Channel, these pipes provided fuel to the invasion forces.

The commander of U.S. forces at Omaha and Utah was General Omar Bradley. By 9:00 a.m. he could see that the assault on Omaha was stalled. Men and equipment crowded the beach as the tide came in. Losses were heavy. Bradley considered giving up on the Omaha sector and switching his remaining troops to the British beaches.

Yet, in that terrible confusion, the American troops were beginning to claw their way off the beaches. Small groups of men cut paths through barbed wire and minefields. They knocked out German positions at close range, slowly inching their way to higher ground. One officer, Colonel George Taylor, yelled "Two kinds of people are going to stay on this beach, the dead and those who are going to die. Now, let's get the hell out of here." Led by men like Taylor, more and more troops pushed their way off the beach.

. . . the American troops were beginning to claw their way off the beaches.

The fighting moved into the countryside and villages beyond the beach. More men and equipment came ashore. As night fell, the Americans held a small foothold extending no more than 2 miles (3.2 km) inland. Roughly 30,000 men had come ashore, at a cost of some 2,500 casualties. And their position was not secure.

Gold, Juno, and Sword Beaches: The Battle Rages On

The British and Canadian forces were led by General Bernard Montgomery. They would land on three beaches: Gold, Juno, and Sword. General Montgomery's troops had several goals for D-Day. From Gold Beach they would push westward to link up with the Americans at Omaha. They would also march inland and, if possible, capture the towns of Bayeux and Caen. The capture of these towns would give the Allies control of key roads. This maneuver would make it harder for the Germans to counterattack. It would also make it much easier for the Allies to break out of the Normandy region into the rest of France. The beaches in the British-Canadian sector were flat and open, unlike the American beaches.

On the other hand, the Anglo-Canadians faced the danger of a counterattack by the tanks of the 21st Panzer Division, positioned around Caen. Also, any German reinforcements immediately rushed to Normandy would come from the east and hit the British and Canadians first. As the troops landed at about 7:30 a.m., the German fire was generally light. Many of the defenders were inexperienced troops. Specialized tanks known as "Funnies" cleared mines and blasted German defenses. Allied troops and tanks pushed inland. At Gold the British fought their way off the beach and headed for Bayeux to the south. Other troops headed west to the town of Port-en-Bessin, a key position between the British and Omaha Beach. By nightfall the Gold beachhead measured nearly 6 miles (10 km) square. However, the British had failed to capture the French towns of Bayeux and Port-en-Bessin.

The Canadians targeted Juno, 5 miles (8 km) east of Gold. After meeting some tough opposition on the beach, they pushed on. By nightfall they had linked up with Gold to the west. However, the Canadians had not been able to capture Caen or link up with the troops at Sword.

The British Second Army, part of the 21st Army Group under General Bernard Montgomery, landed on the Gold, Juno, and Sword beaches of Normandy on D-Day, June 6, 1944.

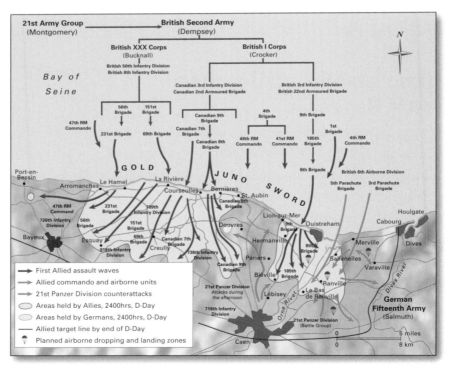

British troops advanced inland from the Normandy beaches. The Allied leadership knew that they would have to move quickly. They needed to gain as much territory as possible before the Germans could organize and react.

On Sword Beach some British troops had a strong fight, while others met almost no opposition. Pushing toward Caen, 8 miles (13 km) away, lead troops met up with British paratroopers holding the Orne bridges. However, when the German 21st Panzer Division counterattacked, the push stopped. At day's end the British were just 3 miles (5 km) from Caen, but that was as far as they got.The landings had taken the Germans by surprise. They rushed troops from other parts of northern France toward the Allied beachhead.

D-Day—the Outcome

D-Day had been a gigantic, risky operation. By the end of June 6, the Allied commanders felt that their gamble had paid off. They had broken through the Atlantic Wall in five places. Some 150,000 men had come ashore, and many more would follow. The Germans' reaction to D-Day had been slow and disorganized. Some German troops had fought hard, but others had given up quickly. Allied casualties, including dead, wounded, and captured, totaled about 10,000 troops. This was half the casualties that Allied leaders had been expecting.

Allied casualties, including dead, wounded, and captured, totaled about 10,000 troops.

However, the invasion was running behind schedule. The American and Anglo-Canadian beaches had not been united. The Allies had not captured Caen and its road hub. Caen was the key to breaking out of Normandy into the heart of France and toward the German border. The element of surprise was now gone. The Allies needed to link their beaches, to extend their perimeter inland, and to organize as reinforcements landed. Many new Allied troops had never seen combat and would soon have to fight veteran German troops being rushed toward the battle. Normandy's battle would grind on for weeks, with heavy casualties on both sides.

▶ After D-Day, Allied forces moved inland from the coasts of France, battling German forces as they went. Allied hopes for an early end to the war faded as the months progressed. Shown in the background is the invasion fleet assisting the landing operations that continued in June 1944.

3 From Normandy to the Ardennes

KEY PEOPLE	KEY PLACES	
🇬🇧 General Bernard Montgomery	Normandy, France	Cherbourg, France
🇺🇸 General Dwight D. Eisenhower	Ardennes, Belgium	Bastogne, Belgium
⊗ Field Marshal Günther von Kluge		Falaise, France
⊗ Adolf Hitler	Caen, France	Antwerp, Belgium
🇺🇸 General George S. Patton		Arnhem, Belgium
🇺🇸 General Omar Bradley		

The Allies faced two major problems in Normandy in June 1944. Despite a steady buildup, their advantages in men and equipment were offset by the terrain and by the quality of the opposition. The German forces were more experienced and were well led at all levels. Many were from elite units that had fought in the east. They faced Allied troops that were entering combat for the first time.

In terms of equipment, the Germans had better tanks, although fewer of them. And the German *Nebelwerfer* artillery piece was known by Allied troops for its devastating fire and screaming projectiles, which earned it the nickname "Moaning Minnies." The Allies had the edge in heavy artillery, but most importantly they had command of the air. Flying constant patrols over the battlefield, they could be radioed onto a target in a matter of minutes. Farther afield, light and medium bombers struck at German units heading for the battlefield. Many of the units arrived late and severely damaged. As losses mounted, the Germans began to move by night whenever possible.

British Failure at Caen

The British narrowly failed to take the inland port of Caen on June 6. They tried again the following day by striking southward. One wing of the attack got bogged down fighting for the village of Cambes. The other wing led by the Canadian 3rd Division ran into a new and formidable opponent, the 12th SS Panzer Division. Known as the *Hitlerjugend*, many of its teenage volunteers were seeing action for the first time, but fought like veterans. The Canadians stopped and were forced to withdraw.

The second British effort to take Caen was a pincer attack by two of Montgomery's veteran units, the 7th Armoured and 51st Highland Divisions. They were supported by naval and air bombarments. The advance opened on June 10, but the Highlanders north of Caen were halted almost immediately.

The disaster at Villers-Bocage ended Montgomery's plan to seize Caen quickly. Also, the element of surprise created on D-Day was gone.

The fate of the armored division to the west was even worse. Pushing toward the village of Villers-Bocage and a gap in the German line, the scouting unit was attacked by the Germans on the first day and the unit could not advance for twenty-four hours. Progress was again slow. However, on the morning of June 13, the lead unit entered the village. It was met by a small force of German tanks, including four Tigers. One of these tanks was commanded by Michael Wittmann, Germany's finest tank commander. He and his men almost single-handedly destroyed the British column in a matter of minutes. The British retreated, and the advance was called off.

The disaster at Villers-Bocage ended Montgomery's plan to seize Caen quickly. Also, the element of surprise created on D-Day was gone. The Germans were feeding fresh units into Normandy. These units were not powerful enough to throw the Allies back across the channel as Hitler demanded. But the Germans could slow the Allied breakout and inflict huge casualties. Caen could now only be taken by a massive, slow assault, certainly not Montgomery's original idea of a lightning advance.

The resources for this new plan seemed to arrive on schedule. Some 500,000 Allied troops were in Normandy by June 17, in part thanks to the Mulberry harbors erected off Gold and Omaha beaches. Then the weather turned. On June 20 violent storms broke out and lasted for three days. Huge quantities of supplies were lost, as well as 800 vessels. Worst of all, the Omaha Mulberry was destroyed, and the Gold Mulberry was damaged. As the flow of supplies fell by 80 percent, it was even more important for the Allies to secure a workable port.

The third effort to take Caen, this time by sweeping southeast 5 miles (8 km) west of the town, was code-named Epsom. Time was short because the Germans were rapidly rushing reinforcements into the area. The attack was delayed for two days by the storm in the channel.

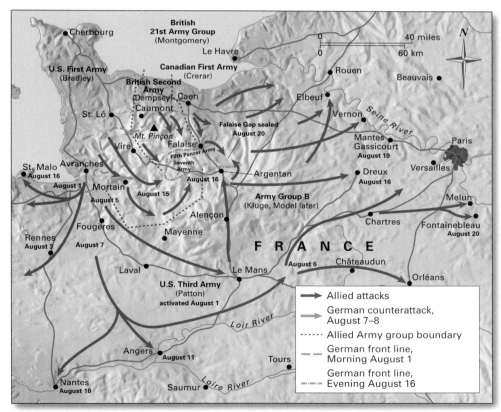

This map shows the Allied breakout from their bridgehead in Normandy in the summer of 1944. Allied progress was slow at first, but the pace quickened at the beginning of August 1944.

When Epsom began, low clouds blocked British air support, while heavy rains and stiff German resistance slowed progress. On June 28, after three days of bitter fighting, British tanks took Hill 112. From there, they could block the main road running southeast from Caen to St. Lo and beat off a counterattack by the II SS Panzer Corps. The taking of Hill 112 was a key moment, since the Germans could not switch reinforcements as easily with the loss of the road. Yet Montgomery, fearing a more organized German backlash, halted Epsom on June 30. Four thousand troops had died.

While General Montgomery was battering away at Caen, the U.S. First Army of General Omar Bradley was improving its position. Troops from Omaha and Gold linked up on June 8, and Omaha and Utah were united after a struggle for Carentan. Bradley's next task was to clear the Cotentin Peninsula, west of Utah, home to the port of Cherbourg. Major General Lawton Collins's U.S. VIII Corps was unleashed. By June 18 it had cut directly across its base to reach the Atlantic coast. Collins, nicknamed "Lightnin' Joe" for his drive and energy, now moved northward toward Cherbourg itself. His troops brushed aside any resistance, and the port surrendered on June 28.

On June 28, after three days of bitter fighting, British tanks took Hill 112.

The Breakout from Normandy

June was a month marked by frustration and disappointment for the Allies. Progress toward Caen had been slow and costly. The Allied timetable was falling behind schedule. The only bright spot was the capture of the port city of Cherbourg. However, its harbor had been destroyed by the Germans. The port could only process 10 percent of the supplies needed to flow through it. It did not become fully operational until late August.

By early July the Allies realized they were not likely to break out from their beachhead by way of Caen. This was confirmed in two days of fighting for the town beginning on July 7. Operation Charnwood opened with 450 British bombers leveling Caen's northern outskirts, followed by an

AFRICAN AMERICANS AT WAR

Many African Americans viewed the war as an opportunity to serve their country while also bringing about the end of discrimination. Although the Selective Service Act of 1940 legislated against discrimination, black recruits in the army were organized in segregated units and trained separately. A large percentage of black soldiers served in noncombat units and many of them remained on home soil. Only three large African-American army units—the 92nd and 93rd Infantry and 2nd Cavalry Divisions—saw combat.

The situation was no better in the other services. Although warships were not segregated for practical reasons, African Americans were usually assigned menial tasks—95 percent served as cooks. In the air force, the majority of African Americans were employed in the support services, such as airfield maintenance. The 99th Fighter Squadron, one of only four African-American combat squadrons, was a notable exception. Formed at Tuskegee, Alabama, it was deployed to the Mediterranean theater in April 1943. Its chief duty was bomber escort. No U.S. bomber was lost in action when escorted by the unit.

The demands of war led to improvements: 5,000 African Americans received commissions. Benjamin O. Davis reached the senior rank of Brigadier General. In early 1945 a program was set up to train African Americans to fight alongside white units in northwest Europe. About 5,000 volunteered.

The peak of African-American service in the army came in September 1944, when 700,000 were serving—a little under 9 percent of the total strength, with a little more than 50 percent serving overseas. A further 165,000 were with the U.S. Navy, 17,000 with the Marines, and 5,000 in the U.S. Coast Guard. However, segregation remained an official policy until 1948.

Anglo-Canadian advance through ruined streets. As the Allies advanced, the Germans inflicted casualties on the attackers, blew up bridges over the Orne River, and established strong defenses on its far bank. With its roads blocked by debris and the bridges destroyed, Caen's potential as a gateway for fast-moving Allied divisions disappeared.

Montgomery's fixation on Caen had cost the British dearly. However, it had one potential benefit that could be exploited if the Allies moved quickly. Since the Germans were moving most of their reserves into battle at the expense of their positions opposing American forces to the west, Bradley's First Army had the opportunity to stage a major offensive.

If successful, Bradley's offensive might lead to capture of Brittany and its ports. However, if the British halted their attacks, then the Germans on the outside of Caen might be switched to fight against Bradley. Bradley's forces outnumbered the Germans two to one at that time.

Bradley's plan, a narrow-front drive between the Atlantic coast and St. Lo, was code-named Cobra. But first Bradley needed about ten days to capture St. Lo before he could move his forces into positions from which to launch Cobra. The solution was for Montgomery to press on against Caen. It was not a great prospect, since intelligence indicated that the Germans had new lines of defense in the area.

Nevertheless, Operation Goodwood began on July 18. Preceded by a massive bombing raid and the firing of some 250,000 artillery and naval shells, the main thrust came to the east of Caen.

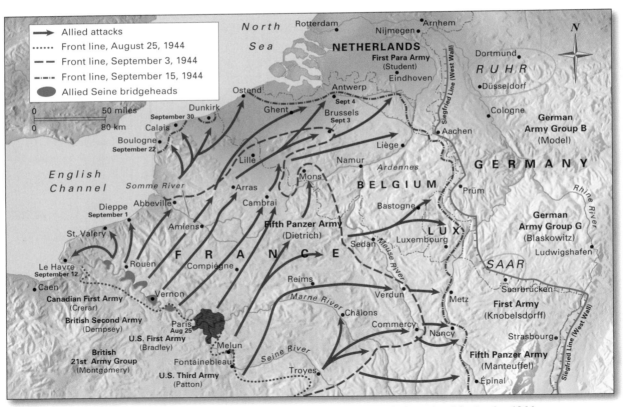

This map shows the Allied advance through France and Belgium in August and September 1944.

The steady progress allowed Montgomery to claim that a breakthrough was imminent. His hopes were dashed over the following three days. An intense thunderstorm on July 21 halted further operations. The Germans were finally pushed back from Caen by a maximum distance of 7 miles (11 km), but at a cost of 6,000 casualties and 400 tanks lost.

General Dwight D. Eisenhower, supreme Allied commander, was aghast at Montgomery's initial optimism. He said: "It has taken 7,000 tons of bombs to gain 7 miles and the Allies can hardly hope to go through France paying a price of 1,000 tons of bombs per mile." Some demanded that Montgomery be fired. Yet, Montgomery backtracked and stated that his talk of a breakthrough had been misinterpreted. Goodwood did succeed in one key sense. The Germans kept two armored divisions from the battle for St. Lo. Those fell into American hands on June 18.

The American troops took two days to batter through what remained of the German lines.

Bradley launched Cobra on July 25, four days late due to the same storm that had ended Goodwood. About 1,500 American bombers paved the way. Some of their bombs fell short, killing or wounding 600 American troops. But the impact on the Germans was great. Lieutenant General Fritz Bayerlain, commander of the elite Panzer Lehr Division, later recalled: "My front line looked like a lunar landscape and at least 70 percent of my troops were out of action—dead, wounded, crazed, or numbed."

The American troops took two days to batter through what remained of the German lines. They had the help of a new piece of equipment. Named after the sergeant who came up with the idea, the Cullin plow was made of cut-up steel defenses from D-Day. Fitted to the front of tanks, it helped the troops bulldoze a path through the terrain's hedgerows.

Eisenhower then placed General George Patton in charge of one of Bradley's corps. He was to drive south into Brittany as quickly as possible. He also asked that Montgomery keep up pressure on the Germans around Caen. Montgomery launched Operation Bluecoat on July 30. This plan drew in German reserves and ended with the successful battle to capture Mount Pinçon on August 6. Patton was freed from facing a major German counterattack. So he drove his men at lightning speed, pushing seven divisions through the gateway to Brittany in just three days.

Fanning out south and west into an area largely abandoned to the French Resistance by scattered German forces, Patton sensed a great opportunity. With the exception of a few ports, Brittany was clear of the enemy. He could switch the bulk of his command eastward, driving them behind the Germans still in Normandy. In the quickly formed plan, Patton would strike eastward and then turn north toward Falaise, while the U.S. First Army pushed eastward. The British would move southward toward Falaise from around Caen. If Patton and the British could join together, then the Germans in Normandy would be surrounded.

The Falaise Pocket

Hitler unknowingly aided the Allied plan. He committed his weakened forces to a counterattack, Operation Lüttich (Liège), near Mortain at the western edge of the pocket around Falaise on August 7–8. It was blunted after some stiff combat, but more importantly, it left the German survivors far from Falaise and their only escape route. The British drive southward from Caen toward Falaise began late on August 7. However, the British drive was slow-paced rather than the required lightning strike. The American advance to the south of the pocket was much more rapid, but they had farther to travel to reach Falaise.

The Commander of the German forces in Normandy, Field Marshal Günther von Kluge, recognized that retreat was the only option. On August 16 he sent a blunt message to Hitler advising him of retreat. Without receiving confirmation from Hitler, Kluge began the withdrawal the same day. The next day Kluge was replaced by Field Marshal Walther Model. Two days later, Kluge committed suicide.

German resistance finally ended on August 22. For Germany, the Falaise Pocket had been a disaster comparable to Stalingrad. The German remaining forces in Normandy were just about annihilated. One-third of the Seventh and Fifth Panzer Armies escaped encirclement, but 10,000 men had been killed and 50,000 taken prisoner. Nine thousand armored vehicles, artillery pieces, and transports had been destroyed or abandoned.

The carnage wrought by Allied artillery and ground-attack aircraft in such a confined space sickened many. Smashed and gutted vehicles, rotting bodies, and carcasses of thousands of transport horses on the narrow roads littered the area. But the battle at Falaise produced strategic gains. The bloody Battle of Normandy was over. With no enemy between them and the German border, the Allies could begin their drive through the heart of France. Even as the fighting died away at Falaise, Patton's Third Army was racing for the line of the Seine River.

The Drive Across France

After Falaise, the Allies struck out across France along a broad front. They brushed aside what little opposition they met. Instead of the inch-by-inch progress of Normandy and heavy casualties, Allied units were covering dozens of miles per day at minimal cost in an exhilarating time. On August 26 Patton's Third Army crossed the Seine River, the only real barrier to its progress in northern France. The U.S. First Army crossed the same river on each side of Paris.

The honor of liberating the French capital was given to the French 2nd Armored Division. Farther north, Anglo-Canadian forces struck out for Belgium and the Netherlands. Canadian troops swept along the coast, capturing small ports and destroying the bases the Germans had used to launch V-1 rockets against southeast England.

A long line of German prisoners march along a field en route to an Allied POW camp in August 1944. When the Falaise Pocket fell, the Allies took 50,000 prisoners. Here the prisoners have British and Canadian escorts who ride alongside in jeeps.

To their south the British Second Army took Brussels, the Belgian capital, on September 3. On the following day they drove into the large port of Antwerp. The speed of the assault prevented the Germans from destroying Antwerp's ports, which the Allies badly needed. However, Antwerp's capture did not bring immediate relief, since it lies 50 miles (80 km) inland. Also, the entrance into the North Sea by way of the Scheldt River along the Belgian–Dutch border was blocked by several German-held islands.

LIBERATION OF PARIS

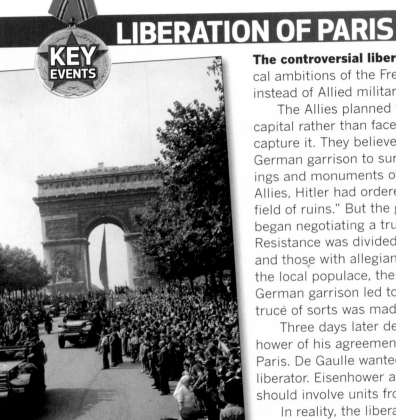

KEY EVENTS

The controversial liberation of Paris reflected the political ambitions of the Free French leader, Charles de Gaulle, instead of Allied military necessities.

The Allies planned to bypass and isolate the French capital rather than face a costly, street-by-street battle to capture it. They believed such a strategy would force the German garrison to surrender and leave the historic buildings and monuments of Paris undamaged. Unknown to the Allies, Hitler had ordered the city to be razed and left "a field of ruins." But the garrison's commander refused and began negotiating a truce with the French Resistance. The Resistance was divided between Communist supporters and those with allegiance to de Gaulle. Tensions between the local populace, the rival Resistance factions, and the German garrison led to street fighting. Nevertheless, a truce of sorts was made on August 19, 1944.

Three days later de Gaulle forcefully reminded Eisenhower of his agreement to let Free French forces occupy Paris. De Gaulle wanted to be seen as France's great liberator. Eisenhower agreed, but insisted that the effort should involve units from all the Allies.

In reality, the liberation of Paris was a race begun and won by the Free French 2nd Armored Division. It entered the city late on August 24 having ignored orders to keep pace with non-French units. De Gaulle attended the first of several victory parades through Paris on August 25. Seen by the French as their liberator, de Gaulle had made great strides toward achieving his political goals.

Operation Market Garden

By early September the western Allies faced a dilemma. The Normandy breakout and drive across northern France had been swift. Also, the forces of Operation Anvil in southern France were advancing rapidly northward. When the Allies linked, the retreating Germans would face a solid line of Allied forces from the Low Countries to the French-Swiss border. Yet Allied progress across northern France would stop, unless the problem of supplying troops was remedied. The Allies agreed that the islands blocking access

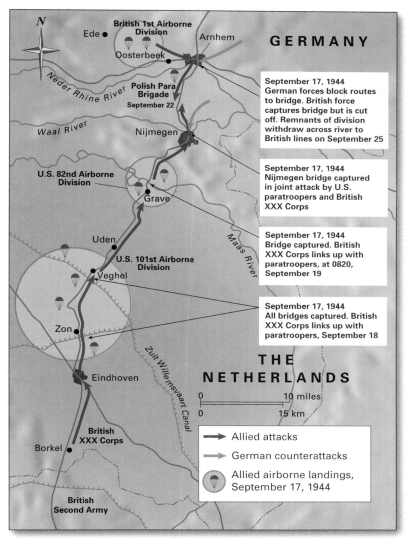

September 17, 1944 German forces block routes to bridge. British force captures bridge but is cut off. Remnants of division withdraw across river to British lines on September 25

September 17, 1944 Nijmegen bridge captured in joint attack by U.S. paratroopers and British XXX Corps

September 17, 1944 Bridge captured. British XXX Corps links up with paratroopers, at 0820, September 19

September 17, 1944 All bridges captured. British XXX Corps links up with paratroopers, September 18

Allied attacks

German counterattacks

Allied airborne landings, September 17, 1944

In the ill-fated Operation Market Garden, Allied airborne troops were to take and hold canals over the Maas, Waal, and lower Rhine rivers. Then Allied armored divisions would provide relief and drive into Germany's Ruhr region.

to Antwerp had to be cleared. However, the debate over how to crush Germany before the end of the year was bitter. Eisenhower finally decided to support Montgomery's plan, code-named Operation Market Garden.

Striking deep into the Ruhr, Germany's economic heartland, to cripple Germany's industry there, the Allied 1st Airborne Corps under Lt. General Frederick Browning, as "Market," would seize key bridges over various canals and the Maas, Waal, and lower Rhine rivers. They would hold them until relieved by "Garden," the British XXX Corps, which would lead the drive into the Ruhr region. Unfortunately, Operation Market Garden was too complex and too hastily enacted. Also, the Allies were unaware that two German panzer divisions had moved into the Arnhem area. Arnhem, the farthest bridge, was also 65 miles (104 km) behind German lines.

In the airborne landings on September 17, the U.S. 82nd and 101st Airborne Divisions secured bridges at Nijmegen and Eindhoven. However, the landings by the British 1st Airborne Division at Arnhem, the farthest bridge, had trouble. The drop zones had to be too far away from the targets and left paratroopers marching to the bridge. Few transport aircraft split up the arrival of the whole division. The delays cost the Allies the element of surprise. German resistance was strong. Only one battalion was able to reach Arnhem and secure the northern end of the bridge. The rest of the division was isolated to the west of the town. The radios did not work, so the Second Army could not communicate with the airborne division's headquarters or the unit at the bridge.

> *The weather worsened. The troops had no reinforcements or supplies.*

The weather worsened. The troops had no reinforcements or supplies. When reinforcements arrived by parachute, many men were killed by ground fire as they descended. The supplies landed in drop zones overrun by Germans. Finally, and most damaging, the Second Army advanced down just one highway flanked by low terrain. Its lead units, confined to the narrow road, were hit by ambushes. The lightning pace that Montgomery had wanted to reach Eindhoven and Nijmegen proved impossible.

Around Arnhem itself the German strategy kept the British division split. At the bridge the intense fighting was house to house. Short of supplies and with a growing casualty list, the paratroopers surrendered on September 21. Troops outside Arnhem defended their ever-shrinking perimeter until September 25. Some escaped back across the Rhine to link up with the Second Army, which was close to the bridge but unable to break through the German line. Browning realized shortly before the battle that the plan was too ambitious—Montgomery had gone "a bridge too far."

The failure of Operation Market Garden meant that the war would not end in late 1944. The Allies were exhausted by their recent advances and further hurt by shortages of supplies. The battle to open Antwerp continued through October and November until Walcheren, the main German-held island at the entrance to the North Sea, was captured in November. Antwerp was not opened until the end of the month.

By the last few weeks of the year the Allied forces had taken up the positions they expected to hold until better weather came in early 1945. All were closing in on the Rhine and the defenses of the Siegfried Line, the

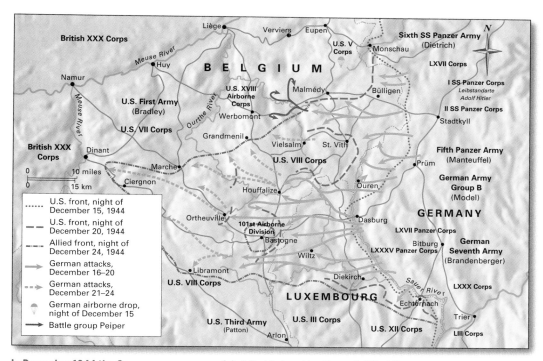

In December 1944 the Germans were successful at first in breaking through Allied lines, as shown on this map. However, the Battle of the Bulge was ultimately a disaster for Hitler.

last barriers between them and Germany. Montgomery's 21st Army Group occupied northern Belgium and a portion of the southern Netherlands. Bradley's U.S. 12th Army Group was close to the German border—in central Belgium, in the Ardennes region of Belgium and Luxembourg, and in a portion of German territory, having breached the Seigfried Line. Patton's Third Army had captured Metz. Between Bradley's armies and the Swiss border lay U.S. general Jacob Devers's Sixth Army Group, which had fought their way from southern France and now stood on the Rhine.

The Battle of the Bulge

With the Allies stalled, Hitler ordered an ambitious counterattack to regain the initiative. The aim of Operation *Wacht am Rhein* (Watch on the Rhine) or Battle of the Bulge, was to punch through the Ardennes. This region was wooded and mountainous—the region where his forces had opened their campaign against France in 1940. Afterward, the German forces would strike northward behind the Allies in the direction of Antwerp.

Hitler's senior commanders feared that the offensive was impracticable and might lead to the loss of the only mobile reserve force that remained. One commander, General Sepp Dietrich, sarcastically identified the acute practical problems: "All I had to do was to cross the river [Meuse], capture Brussels, and then go on to take the port of Antwerp. The snow was waist deep and there wasn't room to deploy four tanks abreast, let alone six armored divisions. It didn't get light until eight and was dark again at four, and my tanks can't fight at night. And all this at Christmastime."

The storm broke on December 16, when twenty-five German divisions advanced on a 60-mile (96-km) front against six weak U.S. divisions. The Allies were caught by surprise. Allied intelligence, the use of English-speaking troops disguised as American personnel, had failed. In addition, a cloud cover masked movement of the German forces. Many American units were overwhelmed or fell back, but scattered groups fought hard, defending key villages, bridges, and crossroads. The Germans expected to capture U.S. supply dumps to help their own fuel shortage. Any delay harmed the German timetable and worsened their fuel crisis.

MASSACRE AT MALMÉDY

In December 1944 Malmédy, a village in the Belgian Ardennes, was the site of the worst massacre of American forces by the Germans during the battle to free western Europe.

Colonel Joachim Peiper, a fanatic Nazi and commander of a battle group of Waffen SS, was responsible. His total ruthlessness was demonstrated at dawn on December 17, when his men gunned down nineteen unarmed American prisoners and then killed another fifty.

Later that day, his troops surprised 125 soldiers as they reached the crossroads at Malmédy. They were disarmed and marched to a nearby field. Two hours later, the unarmed men were machine-gunned by Waffen SS troops. Eighty-six men were killed in cold blood, with a number escaping by pretending to be dead. When news of the massacre reached the U. S. troops, it stiffened their resolved to contain the German offensive.

Even amid the confusion of the first few days, American troops scored some successes. These wins were chiefly on the flanks, where the German advances made only limited headway. The key battle at Bastogne was in the center. It was the hub of the main roads leading to the Meuse and had to be taken quickly if the German advance on Antwerp was to continue.

Its defenders stood firm, forcing the Germans to besiege the town rather than pushing forward to the Meuse. Eisenhower then fed 200,000 reinforcements into the Ardennes in just four days. From December 23 on, clear skies allowed Allied aircraft to pound the Germans. Bastogne was taken on December 26 and the Germans fell back. By the end of January 1945 the bulge had been dealt a final blow.

The Battle of the Bulge was the largest battle fought by American forces in World War II. It was a disaster for Hitler. His forces suffered 100,000 casualties, and huge quantities of matèriel were destroyed or abandoned. His strategic reserve was frittered away in an overly ambitious offensive. Now the Allies would surely be able to push into western Germany when the weather improved. Hitler's commanders would have few resources and little time to prepare. However, the Soviet Union launched an all-out assault on January 12. The Soviet Red Army intended to give no rest to the enemy and to end the war in just forty-five days.

▶ To assist in the Italian campaign, the U. S. Fifth Army (VI Corps) debark tanks from an LST in Italy's Anzio Harbor in January 1944. The Anglo-U.S landings were intended to surprise and to outflank the defenses of the Gustav Line.

4 Italy and the Mediterranean, 1944 to 1945

KEY PEOPLE	KEY PLACES
General Mark Clark	Anzio, Italy
Field Marshal Albert Kesselring	Monte Cassino, Italy
Prime Minister Winston Churchill	Rome, Italy
General Oliver Leese	Po Valley, Italy
General Alphonse Juin	
Major General Lucian Truscott	

By the end of 1943 the Allied 15th Army Group had moved northward from Salerno in southern Italy. But that advance had been blocked by the German-held Gustav Line. This defensive system ran across the center of the Italian peninsula roughly halfway between Rome and Naples, the main point of entry for Allied reinforcements.

The geography of Italy greatly favored the German commander, Field Marshal Albert Kesselring. He directed Army Group C to dig in to exploit this advantage. The Gustav Line made excellent use of rivers running across the Allied line of advance and mountaintops that gave wide fields of fire. A key position was the town of Monte Cassino. German forces blocked the main road along which Lieutenant General Mark Clark's U.S. Fifth and General Oliver Leese's British Eighth Armies were pushing on toward Rome. Since the Allies were advancing through the narrow coastal strip and were hemmed in, Cassino had to be conquered.

The bitter struggle for Cassino opened on January 11, 1944. The French Expeditionary Corps under General Alphonse Juin and the U.S. II Corps attempted to launch a surprise attack in bad weather. The French moved first and managed, after suffering severe casualties, to capture Monte Belvedere, 5 miles (8 km) to the north. The U. S. attack, which began on January 25, secured a bridgehead opposite Monte Cassino but was then stopped in its tracks. Within a few days the Allies realized they would not quickly break through at Cassino. The Allied line advanced only 7 miles (11 km) along the coast, at a cost of 16,000 casualties. But at Monte Cassino the gains could be measured in yards.

Allied Failure at Anzio

With the Allied advance toward Rome blocked along the Gustav Line at Cassino, the Allies planned to land behind the German positions and force the Germans to withdraw northward or face encirclement. The final decision to launch the operation, code-named Shingle, was made in early January 1944. It involved the surprise landing of an Anglo–U.S. expeditionary force at Anzio, a port on the west coast of Italy 60 miles (96 km) from Cassino and about 35 miles (56 km) south of Rome.

Ultra's prediction of light opposition was correct. But Lucas did not take advantage of the element of surprise. Bad weather further delayed the unloading process.

The Allied Ultra intelligence-gathering operation confirmed that there were few German units around Anzio. To draw attention away from the landings, the Allies planned a diversionary assault at Cassino. Major General John Lucas's U.S. VI Corps, part of Clark's Fifth Army, was to carry out the amphibious assault at Anzio. There was little time to work out the details before the landings began on January 22.

Ultra's prediction of light opposition was correct. But Lucas did not take advantage of the element of surprise. Bad weather further delayed the unloading process. Instead of striking out from Anzio, Lucas ordered his troops to dig in. This decision gave the German commander, Kesselring, time to transfer troops to Anzio. The Germans took up positions behind the landing sites, from where they could observe and fire on the beachhead. When Lucas attempted to break out, his forces suffered severe casualties and made little progress.

Feeling that he had the initiative, Kesselring ordered the elimination of the beachhead. Forewarned by Ultra, however, the Allies were able to beat off two major attacks in mid- and late February, in part due to air superiority and naval gunfire support. These limited successes did not save Lucas, who was dismissed and replaced by Major General Lucian Truscott.

Truscott effectively took over the stalemate. He was too weak to break out from Anzio, while Kesselring was not strong enough to push the Allies back into the Mediterranean. For ordinary soldiers the fighting around the beachhead developed into something like trench warfare. Night raids and larger attacks took place, but the men spent much of their day sheltering from snipers, mortar fire, and artillery bombardments. The Allies suffered

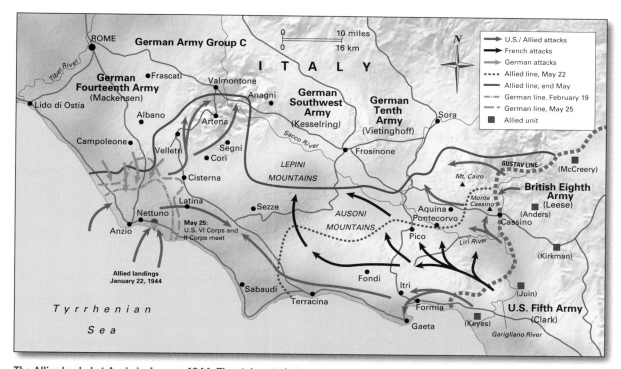

The Allies landed at Anzio in January 1944. The stalemate between the Allies and the German forces lasted until May of that year.

Allied bombers have blown this Nazi motor transport off the road north of Cassino in the 1944 battle. Supplies that never reached the Germans lay strewn below the road.

the greater misery since their positions were still watched by German artillery spotters, who directed bombardments from two huge railroad guns that lobbed 564-pound (256-kg) shells more than 35 miles (56 km). Midget submarines, explosive-filled motorboats, and German aircraft, some fitted with wire-guided gliding bombs, also took their toll on the Allies. The stalemate at Anzio ended in late spring, when the reinforced VI Corps at last pushed out from its perimeter and linked up with the Fifth Army's U.S. II Corps. The irony was that this linkage had been made possible by the ending of the stalemate on the Gustav Line after the costly Allied capture of Monte Cassino.

Cassino was a battle that Anzio was supposed to have made unnecessary. In fact, Cassino finally split the German defenses in southern Italy, forcing Kesselring's withdrawal from Anzio and the abandonment of Rome. Anzio was a lost opportunity for the Allies. Its mishandling cost them dearly—7,000 dead, 36,000 wounded or missing in action, and 44,000 sick or injured casualties. The Germans also lost 40,000 men.

Churchill, who had been the prime mover behind Shingle, summed up the disappointment at the failure to break out from Anzio: "I expected to see a wild cat roaring into the mountains—and what do I find? A whale wallowing on the beaches." However, Anzio did have an impact on future German movements. Kesselring remained convinced that the Allies would launch more amphibious assaults. He frequently held back sizeable forces from the front to deal with any such threat if it arrived.

Battle for Cassino

As the fighting around Anzio continued, the struggle for Cassino to the south reached new intensity. The first attempt to capture the town and its monastery quickly stalled because of winter weather, mountainous terrain, and the German defenses. Nevertheless, with the Anzio operation rapidly collapsing, the Allies had to take Cassino if only to divert German reinforcements from the weak Allied bridgehead to the north.

After another disaster from the U. S. Fifth Army's attempt on the position in January, the Allied commander for this theater, General Harold Alexander, turned to the British Eighth Army under General Oliver Leese. Leese chose New Zealand and Indian troops for the second battle, which was preceded by an aerial bombardment of the monastery. The assault began on February 18 and rapidly broke down. The bombing failed to pave the way for ground troops. Not one German soldier was killed in the raid because not one German soldier was in the monastery. The surprise was lost because the assault units waited an entire day before attacking. Once again, the Allies won little territory at a high cost. Alexander called a halt to the fighting.

Alexander now proposed to attack in strength only, in his words, "after a bombardment worthy of the name."

The attack had failed for two reasons. Only a small number of forces were involved. The preliminary bombardment was also not strong enough. Alexander now proposed to attack in strength only, in his words, "after a bombardment worthy of the name." This new attack began on March 14 and 15, when 600 Allied bombers destroyed both the town and monastery.

Then about 750 artillery pieces firing 200,000 shells followed the attack.

The impact of the bombardment was mixed, even though it was an impressive sight. While many defenders were killed, the survivors turned the ruins into defensive positions. A head-on assault was launched at two points. Once again the attack degenerated into a close-quarters slugging match. Finally, Alexander ended the fighting on March 22. After three costly battles, Cassino clearly was not going to fall without the Allies suffering terrible casualties. However, breaking through the Gustav Line was more important than ever because of the stalemate at Anzio. The solution was to launch a large-scale offensive along the front line involving the U.S. Fifth and British Eighth Armies and the U.S. VI Corps. The offensive would begin at Anzio to switch the focus away from Cassino back to the coastal plain. The new direction would prevent the German defenders from moving reinforcements from one part of their line to another, since they would now face pressure all along their front.

Alexander's ambitious operation to pierce the Gustav Line, break out from Anzio, and capture Rome was code-named Diadem. It opened on May 11. With D-Day close at hand, Diadem was both strategically and politically important. Diadem seemed to be the last chance for the Allied forces in Italy to change the course of the war before the 15th Army Group lost resources to northwest Europe.

The Eighth Army was given the task of breaking the Gustav Line to the north of Cassino. The U.S. Fifth Army attempted the main breakthrough along the coast, and was led by Juin's French Expeditionary Corps. In a spectacular feat, the Corps smashed through the Gustav Line on the southern edge of the Liri Valley. On the coast itself the U.S. II Corps also made steady progress. In the center the Polish Corps, under the command of General Wladyslaw Anders, faced a stiff fight for Monte Cassino that produced heavy casualties on both sides. Nevertheless, the monastery was finally captured on May 17 and 18. Seven days later, troops from Anzio linked up with II Corps.

With D-Day close at hand, Diadem was both strategically and politically important.

GENERAL WLADYSLAW ANDERS

General Wladyslaw Anders was the commander of the Polish II Corps that after a bitter struggle finally captured Monte Cassino on May 18 and 19. He later recalled the horrors he witnessed.

There were enormous dumps of unused ammunition and here and there heaps of land mines. Corpses of Polish and German soldiers, sometimes entangled in a deathly embrace, lay everywhere, and the air was full of the stench of rotting bodies. Crater after crater pitted the sides of the hills, and scattered over them were fragments of uniforms and tin helmets, tommy guns, Spandaus, Schmeissers, and grenades.

Of the monastery itself there remained only an enormous heap of ruins and rubble, with here and there some broken columns. Only the western wall, over which two flags flew, was still standing. A cracked church bell lay on the ground next to an unexploded shell of the heaviest caliber and on shattered walls and ceilings fragments of paintings and frescoes could be seen. Priceless works of art, sculpture, pictures, and books lay in the dust and broken plaster.

Extract taken from Anders's war memoirs, *An Army in Exile*, Macmillan, 1949.

The Fall of Rome

Diadem achieved its first objective of breaking the Gustav Line and linking up with the Anzio beachhead. The next phase—to trap Kesselring's forces—was a marked failure. Originally, Clark's Fifth Army was to breach the Gustav Line and to swing around behind the Germans before they could retreat. This maneuver would trap the Germans between the Fifth Army and the British Eighth Army. Freeing Rome was secondary to encircling the enemy.

Instead, Clark pushed directly northward to capture Rome, with which he was fixated, rather than swinging eastward. Clark's forces were occasionally checked by small German rear guards placed to slow their drive on Rome. However, Clark's forces did not battle for the capital since it had been abandoned by the Germans. American units entered Rome, the first Axis capital to fall to the Allies, on June 4. Three days later, Alexander attempted to resume his pursuit of Kesselring. The Germans were withdrawing, and their casualties mounted as they were harried by Allied airpower.

Churchill was still convinced that the liberation of Italy would set the scene for a major drive into southern Europe. He proposed a knockout blow south of the Alps in 1944. This would ensure that Italy remain a major theater of operations. Another plan called for the transfer of forces away from Alexander for an amphibious assault against southern France.

Operation Dragoon, in mid-August, would support the imminent D-Day landings. Many senior American commanders believed that Dragoon, rather than a drive into northern Italy, offered the best support for the Normandy invasion. Churchill had to back down. Between June 11 and July 22 Alexander gave up three U.S. and five French divisions—a large portion of his 15th Army Group—for the attack on southern France.

Assaulting the Gothic Line

At the same time, Kesselring had managed to slow the Allied pursuit enough to reestablish a new defensive line across the Italian peninsula.

Two lines of soldiers march along Italy's Highway 6, the famed "Road to Rome," in 1944.

Known as the Gothic Line, it meandered for 200 miles (320 km) from just north of Lucca to the coast just south of Pesaro. Once again the Gothic Line allowed Kesselring to demonstrate his skills at defensive warfare. The focus of the Italian campaign now switched from the west coast, through Cassino and Anzio to the fallen Rome, to the Adriatic coast in the east. The military explanation was that the area around Pesaro was less mountainous and therefore better suited for tanks, in which the Allies had an overwhelming superiority. Also, the recent transfers of forces away from the Italian campaign had fallen on Clark's command. It was clearly the weaker of the two armies available to Alexander. Thus any offensive operation to pierce the Gothic Line and sweep into the valley of the Po River were to be led by the Eighth Army. The Fifth Army would play a supporting role.

THE DEATH OF MUSSOLINI

KEY EVENTS

In his final days Benito Mussolini, the Italian dictator, was little more than a puppet controlled by Hitler. His death came at the hands of his countrymen.

Mussolini's final days bore little resemblance to those he had enjoyed at the height of his power. He had been dismissed by King Victor Emmanuel III on July 23, 1943. Mussolini was arrested, but his time in prison was short. He was freed by a German glider-borne operation on September 12, shortly after Italy announced an armistice with the Allies. Hitler's motives for sanctioning the operation, code-named Oak, were twofold. First, he had a genuine regard for Mussolini; second, the Italian dictator was a valuable figurehead to lead the new Nazi-inspired Italian Social Republic that was created in the north of the country. This regime was merely small cover of Germany's absolute occupation of the region.

By this stage Mussolini's former dynamism was gone. He seemed to accept his new role passively, although it gave him neither power nor authority. His survival rested on Hitler's patronage, but this favor evaporated as Germany came ever closer to defeat in the spring of 1945. With the Allies fast approaching his headquarters at Gargano on Lake Garda, Mussolini attempted to flee to Switzerland with his mistress, Clara Petacci. They were intercepted by pro-Allied Italian partisans on April 26 and shot two days later. Their corpses were then taken to Milan and hung upside down in one of the city's squares. News of this public humiliation convinced Hitler to choose suicide and the burning of his own corpse rather than to suffer a fate similar to Mussolini's.

The offensive also had political dimensions. The British were furious with the publicity Clark had gained for both himself and for his mostly American forces from the capture of Rome. They saw a major British-led victory in northern Italy as a way to regain the limelight.

Leese proposed the Pesaro operation, later code-named Olive, to Alexander on August 4. The Pesaro operation was another strategic error, since Olive committed only part of the 15th Army Group to attack the Gothic Line. Leese had understated the importance of west-to-east rivers and ridges blocking his line of advance along the east coast. Kesselring had fortified the rivers. Allied air raids had destroyed the bridges. Unusually heavy fall rains had turned the rivers into raging torrents. Moreover, Hitler personally ordered the reinforcement of Army Group C, despite the pressures he was facing on both the eastern and western fronts.

The Pesaro operation was another strategic error. . .

It took about two weeks to transfer the Eighth Army to the east coast—an impressive feat. The maneuver involved thousands of vehicles and the construction of forty sectional Bailey bridges to replace those destroyed by the retreating Germans or Allied aircraft. The attack began on August 25, and it made encouraging gains. The infantry—British, Canadian, Indian, and Polish—captured several enemy hilltop positions. Then the tanks moved forward to exploit the advantage. However, the armor moved slowly on the region's poor and twisting roads. Later the tanks ground almost to a halt when heavy rains turned the routes into heavy mud. The resort of Rimini, a few miles beyond the Gothic Line, fell on September 22, but there the Eighth Army's advance stalled. To the west Clark's Fifth Army advanced across the Arno River toward Bologna. It also pierced the Gothic Line at several points, but the attacks suffered from worsening weather and counterattacks by German and Italian units that remained loyal to Mussolini. By mid-December both Allied armies had halted their operations and dug in to ride out a bad winter.

During the winter of 1944 to 1945, both sides shuffled their commands. Leese was moved to the Far East, and command of the Eighth Army went to General Richard McCreery. Alexander was promoted to supreme commander in the Mediterranean. Clark took over his role as head of the 15th Army Group. Truscott, in charge of the Anzio drive and a key figure in Operation Dragoon, assumed command of the U. S. Fifth Army. On the German side Kesselring was moved to northwest Europe. His replacement, General Heinrich Vietinghoff, was given strict no-retreat orders by Hitler.

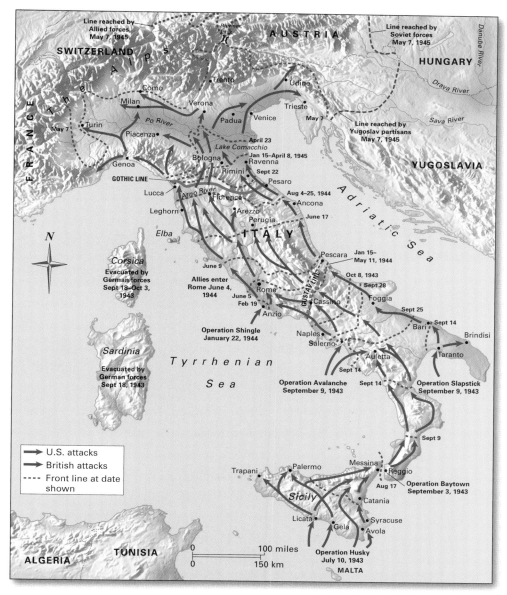

At great human cost, the Allies finally took Italy in 1945.

Into the Po Valley

The winter showed that both Allied and Axis forces were preparing for more fighting. The frontline German forces, nineteen divisions holding a line of about 135 miles (216 km), strengthened their defenses and built up supplies of ammunition and equipment. They faced constant attacks on their lines of communication in northern Italy by Allied aircraft, an operation code-named Strangle. They also suffered from raids by Italian partisans. Behind them lay a reserve of ten Axis divisions that were to guard Italy's borders and prevent a possible amphibious assault around Venice.

For the Allies, winter brought good and bad news. On the positive side, specialized equipment, such as bulldozers, flame-thrower tanks, and amphibious vehicles, arrived from northwest Europe. This equipment would help spearhead a proposed drive across the rivers, lagoons, and swamps north of Rimini in the region of Romagna. On the negative side, 15th Army Group lost some of its divisions to other operations. Three were sent to Greece to intervene in a civil war that had just begun, while its Canadian Corps was transferred to the Netherlands.

On the positive side, specialized equipment, such as bulldozers, flame-thrower tanks, and amphibious vehicles, arrived from northwest Europe.

The Allied operation was complex but imaginative. First there was to be a feint, or misleading action, toward Venice by way of the Romagna using the newly arrived amphibious assault vehicles. This assault was designed to take Lake Comacchio and to confirm to the Germans their belief that larger Allied forces would land along the east coast. The intent of the assault was to prevent the Germans from committing their reserves elsewhere. However, this misdirection was not the whole point of the Comacchio attack. The attack was also to protect an advance by the Eighth Army toward Bologna, which was also the chief target for the U.S. Fifth Army. If Bologna, a center of road and rail links running east–west and north–south across northern Italy, fell to this pincer attack, then the two German armies would be isolated from each other. The operation opened on April 9 and 10. Allies bombed German frontline positions in the Argenta

ITALIAN PARTISANS

STRATEGY & TACTICS

After the Italian armistice in 1943, partisan bands emerged in the north of the country to aid the Allied war effort.

The partisans were of many beliefs, including ex-Fascist soldiers, monarchists, Catholics, socialists, and Communists. But they worked together to create a joint command in 1944. The various groups, 100,000 strong by the end of the year, were based in mountainous areas. They were also active in cities, where they launched raids on German lines of communication. They also aided escaping Allied prisoners of war, carried out assassinations, and damaged installations. Their weapons and equipment came from Allied air drops.

The German response to the partisans included sweeps against their bases and brutal reprisals against civilians. A major German counteroffensive in late 1944 came close to smashing the partisan movement, although the movement revived as the war entered its final phase. Horrific acts against civilians were widespread. At Marzabotto near Bologna, for example, SS troops leveled the town and killed 1,600 civilians and 226 partisans during October. In all, approximately 40,000 Italian partisans and civilians were killed during the course of Germany's antiguerilla operatons.

gap, between Comacchio and the high ground inland. As Comacchio's islands were cleared, the Eighth Army's pincer drive on Argenta itself rolled forward. Truscott's Fifth Army advanced on Bologna on April 14 against stubborn German resistance. With twin Allied blows supported by overwhelming airpower, German defenses crumbled. Bologna fell to Polish troops on April 21. Two days later units from the two Allied armies linked up at Finale Emilia to the north of the city.

In the past the Allies had failed to capitalize on such breakthroughs, thereby allowing the Germans to retreat to new positions. For this assault, however, the Germans did not gain new positions. Vietinghoff had already ordered a wholesale withdrawal to the north bank of the Po, in defiance of Hitler's order. But the move proved almost impossible. The Allied air attacks had destroyed many bridges. Long columns of troops attempting to flee blocked those bridges that survived.

The discipline and cohesion of the German survivors melted away as Allied ground forces harried them on their way. By April 23 Hitler's Army Group C was shattered. In two weeks of action, Allied casualties amounted to 16,500 men, a figure dwarfed by 22,000 Germans killed or wounded and a further 35,000 taken prisoner. With little to oppose them, the Allies fanned out across northern Italy. One by one, northern Italy's great cities were liberated. Allies entered Venice and Milan, where the recently executed body of Mussolini was on display, on April 29. Liberation of Trieste and Turin followed on May 2, the day that the remnant of German Army Group C finally surrendered.

Italy: A Necessary Campaign?

The Italian campaign remains controversial. The British suffered 189,000 casualties and the Americans about 123,000, while German losses amounted to 435,000. The fighting had more impact on the German forces than those of the Allies. However, Italy was never more than a sideshow to Hitler. He committed most of his armed forces to the eastern and western fronts, not to Italy, which he defended on a shoestring.

Consequently, the Allies were never going to destroy the German army in Italy. Churchill was determined to deliver a knockout blow against

OPERATION STRANGLE

KEY EVENTS

In the spring of 1944 the Allies launched a supreme effort to block the flow of supplies to German forces in northern Italy. In March of 1944 Allied aircraft began the supporting operation, code-named Strangle, against the German forces holding the Gustav Line in northern Italy. Operation Strangle was to sever the supply lines that fed the Gustav Line before an attack by Allied ground forces. U. S. and British aircraft ranged far and wide over northern Italy, targeting road and rail lines. Despite dropping thousands of bombs, however, the Allies did not entirely stop the flow of supplies. Germans were replacing the transportation losses with those commandeered from the Italians. The Germans also conducted resupply missions under cover of darkness. Nevertheless, Operation Strangle became a model for the more successful and similar raids that isolated Normandy both before and during the invasion of June 1944.

British troops on Monte Cassino display a cartoon of Hitler in May 1944.

Germany by way of Italy. But this approach was never a real possibility—partly because of the terrain, which supported the defenders, and partly because the United States wanted to deliver the decisive blow by way of northwest Europe. Thus the fighting in Italy was conducted with scarce resources. Units and equipment were withdrawn for D-Day and landings in southern France. The Allies did learn from the Italian campaign, since the Allies conducted three amphibious assaults—Sicily, Salerno, and Anzio—that provided experience for the coming operations in France.

▶ In 1944 the Russians began to reverse their losses and turn the course of the war against the Germans. These Soviet Red Army troops advance on German positions near the city of Minsk, one of the last Soviet cities to be liberated from German invaders.

5 The Eastern European Front, 1944

<table>
<tr><td colspan="2">KEY PEOPLE</td><td colspan="2">KEY PLACES</td></tr>
<tr><td></td><td>Field Marshal Walther Model</td><td></td><td>Soviet Union (Russia)</td></tr>
<tr><td></td><td>Adolf Hitler</td><td></td><td>Soviet Union (Ukraine)</td></tr>
<tr><td></td><td>Joseph Stalin</td><td></td><td>Finland</td></tr>
<tr><td></td><td>Field Marshal Erich von Manstein</td><td></td><td>Leningrad (St. Petersburg), Russia</td></tr>
<tr><td></td><td>Marshal Vasily Zhukov</td><td></td><td>Korsun, Ukraine</td></tr>
<tr><td></td><td></td><td></td><td>Warsaw, Poland</td></tr>
</table>

By the end of 1943 the Red Army had gained the military initiative on the eastern front. German forces struggled to hold on to what remained of the gains they had made in 1941 and 1942 in order to keep the Red Army far from Berlin. However, Hitler was growing concerned about possible Anglo–U.S. landings in the west that would threaten Germany's industrial areas. He directed more and more resources to this war zone.

Despite his generals' concerns about weakness on the eastern front, Hitler believed that forces there could afford to give ground without endangering the Third Reich. In contrast, Stalin had great plans for 1944. The Red Army had already liberated half of the Soviet territory that Germany had occupied at the height of its successes. Now he planned to free the remainder by launching attacks in the north, center, and south.

The Liberation of Leningrad (St. Petersburg)

The Red Army's operations began outside Leningrad (St. Petersburg) in mid-January 1944. The Red Army's maneuvers involved the armies of the Leningrad, Volkhov, and 2nd Baltic fronts. The commander of Germany's Army Group North, Field Marshal Georg von Küechler, recognized that his units were too weak to hold a front stretching 500 miles (800 km).

In late December 1943 he had requested to withdraw to a position that would reduce his front by 60 miles (96 km). Hitler rejected the proposal, because he feared that any withdrawal might encourage Finland. If a withdrawal occurred, Hitler felt that the more isolated Finland would seek an armistice with the Soviet Union.

So, when the Leningrad and Volkhov fronts were attacked by Soviet forces on January 14, 1944, they easily cut through the flanks of the opposing Eighteenth Army. On January 27 the Volkhov Front passed over the Moscow–Leningrad railroad, linking the Soviet Union's two most important cities for the first time since 1941. Stalin declared the liberation of Leningrad, which had been under attack for almost 900 days.

Hitler's response was to replace Küechler with Field Marshal Walther Model. Model received two extra divisions to aid his operations. These were clearly not enough troops to stabilize the situation. Model, unlike Küechler, convinced Hitler to allow a withdrawal to a zone around Lake Ilmen and Lake Peipus.

The Soviets attacked so relentlessly that Model was forced to fall back farther than intended. The operation took place between mid-February and mid-March. Although successful, the operation's outcome meant that the Germans had been pushed back from the gates of Leningrad. Spring thaws brought the fighting to a temporary halt.

The Battle of Korsun

The main thrust of the Soviet winter offensive was directed against the German Army Group South, commanded by Field Marshal Erich von Manstein. Made up of seventy-three weak divisions, the Group South held positions in the western Ukraine along 650 miles (1,040 km) of the southern section of the eastern front. The Red Army, under Marshal Vasily Zhukov, used the 1st, 2nd, 3rd, and 4th Ukrainian fronts. The initial onslaught, led by General N. F. Vatutin's 1st Ukrainian Front, took on Germany's Fourth Panzer Army, holding the northern flank of Army Group South. The Soviet forces smashed through the German lines in late December 1943.

By early January 1944 the Red Army was closing in on the old Soviet–Polish border. Although other Soviet fronts made less progress, Manstein was aware of the potential threat of being encircled. He had two options. He could transfer some of the troops that were holding a vast bend in the Dnieper River, but this move would leave remaining units open to a similar attack. He could request reinforcements from outside his group.

Although Manstein did move some troops, he made no immediate decision. In early 1944 the field marshal met Hitler to argue for a withdrawal from the Dnieper bend and a move to positions along the Bug River to the west. Such a withdrawal would abandon Crimea, which was part of the front line held by Field Marshal Paul von Kleist's Army Group A.

Manstein found little to cheer him after his meeting with Hitler.

Hitler flatly refused to consider this request. He also refused a transfer of troops. Hitler argued that the Dnieper bend contained minerals vital to Germany's war effort. He also knew that evacuating Crimea might lead to Bulgaria leaving the Axis alliance. The movement of forces from Army Group North in the Baltic States would give the Soviet Union control of the Baltic. Then, Finland might seek peace and thereby threaten the flow of iron ore supplies to Germany from Sweden. Manstein found little to cheer him after his meeting with Hitler. Although the Soviet attacks were slowing, a crisis was developing around Korsun. An early spring thaw made movement difficult. Soviet forces were poised to launch a pincer attack against a salient (or bulge) in the line.

The bulge opened on January 25. By early February the Soviet forces encircled the 56,000 German defenders. The Germans faced overwhelming forces in the depths of winter and were short of supplies. Still, Hitler ordered the men trapped in the Korsun Pocket to hold fast. Reserves were

WALTHER MODEL

Walther Model (*on left*)

Field Marshal Walther Model (1891-1945) was a career army officer. He was considered one of Hitler's best generals. Model was an officer of enormous will. His motto was "Can't that be done faster?" He won a rapid promotion during the invasion of the Soviet Union in 1941.

As the war turned against Germany, he retained Hitler's respect. Hitler sent him to fix the most impossible situations. Model was usually successful and earned the nickname of the "Führer's Fireman." Model survived the German defeat at Kursk in 1943 and in later battles was even able to undertake strategic withdrawals. This was done despite Hitler's prohibition against doing any kind of retreat.

In 1944 Model was made a field marshal. In August 1944 Model was transferred to western Europe to stop the breakout of the Allies from Normandy. He failed, but his later defeat of the Allied Operation Market Garden confirmed his fine leadership qualities.

After the German defeat in the Ardennes in December 1944, Model committed suicide rather than surrender with his troops.

marshaled for a major counterattack that Hitler believed would relieve the troops and also push the Red Army back over the Dnieper.

The planned counterattack never developed. It took time to transfer units from elsewhere. When they arrived in early February, their progress was delayed by the sudden thaw. The only available option was for the troops to break out from the pocket. Although some 30,000 men were able to withdraw, the remainder were hemmed in by swollen rivers.

One Soviet commentator described the final moments of the fighting on February 18: "Hundreds and hundreds of cavalry were hacking at them with their sabers, and massacred the Fritzes [a nickname for German troops] as no one had ever been massacred by cavalry before. There was no time to take prisoners. It was the kind of carnage that nothing could stop until it was over."

After Korsun, a pause in the fighting allowed the Soviet fronts in Ukraine to reorganize. Both sides waited for the ground to harden. The Red Army, taking the initiative once again, launched parallel drives against Army Groups South and A on March 5. Zhukov, now commanding the 1st Ukrainian Front, was able to trap Manstein's First Panzer Army. Kleist ordered his Sixth Panzer Army to withdraw to avoid being trapped between the Bug and Dniester rivers.

These withdrawals infuriated Hitler, and on March 30 he met the two field marshals. After presenting both with high honors, he dismissed them. Manstein was replaced by Model and Kleist by General Ferdinand Schörner. In April, to mask the disasters that had befallen Army Groups South and A, they were renamed Army Groups North and South Ukraine. The two new commanders arrived at the front at the same time as the attacks by Zhukov and Konev were winding down

Crimea Freed

Soviet successes at Korsun and elsewhere in Ukraine further isolated the German Seventeenth Army, which was part of Schörner's new command holding out in Crimea. The attack to liberate the peninsula opened on April 8 and involved the 4th Ukrainian Front striking south though the isthmus that linked Crimea with Russia proper. Three days later the Independent Coastal Army broke out westward from Crimea's east coast.

The German and Romanian forces were unable to stem the Soviet tide. They retreated to preprepared defense lines around Sevastopol. Hitler initially refused all requests to evacuate the trapped troops and only relented on May 9. By that time, it was too late to marshal the resources for a complete withdrawal. Some 27,000 troops from the Seventeenth Army did escape from Crimea, but around 120,000 had been killed or captured.

As the Soviet army advanced toward Sevastopol in the Crimea, the German Seventeenth Army withdrew. Hitler's failure to rescue his forces led to the deaths of 120,000 German troops.

Finland Seeks an End to the War

Finland had joined in Germany's attack on the Soviet Union in 1941. Its aim was to regain territory lost in the Russo–Finnish War. But by late 1942 Hitler was clearly unable to deliver a knockout blow. Finland's war effort was bolstered by German troops in the north and by supplies flowing into the country by way of Estonia, but the country was geographically isolated from its powerful ally. It was becoming more so as German armed forces were slowly cleared from the region. The Finnish leadership tried to reach secret terms with Stalin. Discussions broke down in February 1944, because of Soviet demands for reparations and territory.

Stalin decided to settle the matter through military action. On June 9 General L. Govorov's Leningrad Front struck the Finnish forces stationed on a 10-mile (16-km) sector between the Gulf of Finland and Lake Ladoga. He pierced their defenses and pushed them back 5 miles (8 km). Over the following days the Finns were pushed back elsewhere. By early August they were left holding positions along the new Russo–Finnish border. By this stage the Germans were in crisis, and the Finns opened negotiations that would lead to an end of hostilities with the Soviets in early September.

Army Group Center Shattered

German losses were severe in the first five months of 1944. Hitler still commanded roughly 2.2 million men in the east split between a number of army groups. Despite territorial losses in Ukraine, the front line was still 550 miles (880 km) from Berlin. He and his generals believed that the Red Army would start offensive operations again in the summer, but they debated over where the main attack would be. They settled on the sections held by Army Groups North and South Ukraine. The Germans believed that Stalin would want to capitalize on recent successes in the area.

They were correct, but the Germans did not fully consider the military situation. The Soviet victories in Ukraine also had a negative effect on Field Marshal Ernst Busch's Army Group Center. The retreats there created a large bulge in the line to the east and south of Minsk that left the army group of 700,000 men vulnerable. Busch's weakness increased in May when 90 percent of his tanks and many other vehicles were transferred to Army Group North Ukraine.

The Red Army was now a well-led, confident, experienced force.

On the Soviet side, Zhukov recognized the weakness of Busch's position. In early May 1944 the Soviets began the groundwork for Operation Bagration, designed to smash the German Army Group Center and rupture the eastern front. The Red Army was now a well-led, confident, experienced force. The Soviets also had an overwhelming numerical superiority over the Germans in manpower and weaponry. So Zhukov launched a summer offensive all along the eastern front in a staggered effort.

First, the Red Army would launch the main effort in the center of a line north of the Pripet Marshes at the Russian, Polish, and Latvian borders. Second, other fronts were massed to clear the Baltic states of Estonia, Latvia, and Lithuania. Third, there was a similar effort to clear southern Poland.

In the summer of 1944 Hitler finally had to face the consequences of his earlier military and political failures. In 1940 he had failed to crush Britain. In December 1941 he had declared war on the United States. He did not defeat the Soviet Union in 1941 to 1942. As a result, Hitler was fighting a war on two European fronts. The Allies were ready to launch assaults on western Europe and on the eastern front. The Soviet assault on Army Group Center opened on the night of June 19. Partisans struck successfully

In 1944 the Red Army continued its advances against German forces in the Baltic region. General Busch's Army Group Center could not withstand the attacks. Hitler fired Busch, replacing him with Model.

against its lines of communication and left it isolated. The main ground attack opened on June 22, when the 1st Baltic and 1st Belorussian fronts launched a pincer attack to the north and south of Vitebsk, one of the fortified areas held by the Third Panzer Army.

The Soviets had immense resources available for these attacks because the Soviet economy had been successful in moving to a war footing between 1941 and 1943. The Soviet military effort in the center theater alone involved 166 infantry divisions, 31,000 artillery pieces, more than 5,000 tanks, and 6,000 aircraft. Nazi Germany could not match those totals of equipment and manpower. The Soviet Union also had the resources to quickly replace its losses. Germany did not. Germany's industrial centers and transportation infrastructure were under Allied attack and they had a much smaller pool of manpower for replacements.

The Soviets had immense resources available for these attacks . . .

As the German generals had feared, the Red Army broke through the positions on either side of Vitebsk. Requests by the German commander to withdraw were initially rejected by Hitler. He finally agreed to a partial evacuation on June 24. His delay brought destruction to the Panzer Army, allowing the Soviet army to make a move deep into the lines.

The story of Vitebsk was repeated on Army Group Center's front. Marshal Konstantin Rokossovsky's 1st Belorussian Front crushed units from the Ninth Army holding Bobruysk. They killed 18,000 and captured 16,000 of the fortified area's defenders by June 29. The Red Army also crushed parts of the German Fourth Army holding the fortified areas of Mogilev and Orsha. Survivors had to fight their way westward under attack by both Red Army units and local partisan bands.

By June 28 the Red Army had punched through 180 miles (290 km) of the eastern front and smashed the three armies that made up Busch's command. Hitler had to accept that the Soviet attacks against Army Group Center were causing great damage. His response to the crisis was typical. Hitler fired Busch, replacing him with Model, and ordered the redeployment of forces from Army Groups North and North Ukraine. These transfers took some time to complete.

THE JULY BOMB PLOT

Several attempts on Hitler's life were made both before and during the war. On July 20, 1944, one was almost successful. Senior military officers, aristocrats, and career diplomats had begun to oppose Hitler, as Germany's war effort crumbled. Because Hitler wanted to fight to the bitter end, only his removal would save Germany from destruction. By summer 1944 they thought that Hitler had lost the popular support of the people and the armed forces and was being kept in power by the SS and the Gestapo.

Operation Valkyrie, the code name of the assassination plan, was devised and carried out by Claus Schenk von Stauffenberg. He was a military officer from an aristocratic family. A staff position brought Stauffenberg in frequent contact with Hitler. On July 20 Stauffenberg attended a meeting at Hitler's headquarters. He placed an explosive-filled briefcase under the table. Moments later the bomb exploded.

Hitler survived the bomb. A solid oak table diffused most of the blast. Staffenberg was arrested and executed. Over the following weeks, anyone connected with Valkyrie was rounded up and executed. Two field marshals, Kluge and Rommel, committed suicide, reinforcing Hitler's belief that his army's commanders opposed him. From then on, Hitler distrusted their often sound advice.

At the same time, Army Group Center was wilting under the Soviet attacks. By July 8 the Red Army had killed or captured 285,000 German troops and destroyed or overrun vast amounts of equipment. In celebration of the victory, the Soviets marched huge parades of prisoners through Moscow's streets, with great psychological effect. The complete liberation of Soviet territory was close at hand.

In celebration of the victory, the Soviets marched huge parades of prisoners through Moscow's streets, with great psychological effect.

Model struggled to stabilize the eastern front. He did gain Hitler's permission to abandon the plan to hold fortified areas at all costs. Stalin took advantage of the confusion. He ordered his frontline commanders to broaden attacks that were moving the front westward 15 miles (24 km) each day. The 1st, 2nd, and 3rd Belorussian fronts struck into the northern and central regions of eastern Poland. The 1st Baltic Front drove to the northwest to trap Army Group North, which was occupying Latvia, Lithuania, and Estonia.

The Red Army Enters the Baltic States

The 1st Baltic Front moved rapidly northward, while three other fronts, the 2nd Baltic, 3rd Baltic, and Leningrad, prepared to launch assaults into Latvia and Estonia from the east. Army Group North's commander, Model, asked for permission to withdraw, since some of his troops had been transferred to support Army Group Center. Hitler refused because he was afraid that Finland would be further isolated and would try again to make peace with the Soviet Union. Hitler fired Model on July 2. Model's replacement, General Hans Friessner, agreed with Model about withdrawal. So Hitler replaced Friessner with General Ferdinand Schörner.

Despite his impeccable Nazi credentials, which made him a favorite of Hitler, Schörner was still unable to save the situation. In late July the 3rd Baltic and the Leningrad fronts opened their offensives against Schörner's overstretched command. In August the Soviets pressed on and left Schörner with a 20-mile (32-km) corridor along the Baltic coast with which to link his command with Army Group Center. The situation was critical. Schörner's thirty divisions faced eighty Soviet divisions, but they were not wholly cut off. Some supplies were brought in by German warships,

> *Despite his impeccable Nazi credentials, which made him a favorite of Hitler, Schörner was still unable to save the situation.*

whose guns also gave much-needed support to the trapped army group. The 1st Baltic Front did not sever the corridor in September, but it turned westward into northern Lithuania and captured the Baltic port of Memel in October.

The fall of Memel forced Army Group North to abandon Estonia and eastern Latvia. The German troops retreated to the Courland Peninsula in northern Latvia, where they remained until the end of the war, despite evacuation attempts in May 1945. The loss of Estonia, however, had much wider implications for the future. Its ice-free ports had been sending supplies and troops from Germany to Finland. With this crucial supply line severed, the Finns were effectively isolated. On September 2 Finland signed an armistice with the Soviet Union.

Advance into Poland

During mid-July the Soviets also unleashed Konev's 1st Ukrainian Front against Germany's Army Group North Ukraine, which was holding positions in southern Poland east of the Bug River. Once again, the Red Army had great superiority both on the ground and in the air because Hitler had moved some of the forces from Army Group North Ukraine to help stabilize Army Group Center's front. The Soviet offensive opened on July 13 with two attacks. One was against the German Fourth Panzer Army around Lutsk and the other was against the First Panzer Army in the south of Poland. The Red Army tanks rapidly pierced the German front line. This forced the troops holding Hitler's fortified zones to fight their way across the Bug River. Some escaped, but many did not.

The Soviet army advanced through Poland in July and August 1944. The front lines of the Red Army reached the outskirts of Warsaw, the capital of Poland, by the end of the month.

THE WARSAW UPRISING

In August 1944 the Polish Home Army in Warsaw rose against the German garrison. The incident sparked a controversial episode that soured relations between Stalin and western Allies.

The uprising was part of a wider operation, code-named Tempest. It began in January and was designed to harass the Germans as they retreated westward through the country. Tempest had a political motive. The exiled Polish leadership wanted to install a legitimate nationalist government before Stalin could install a pro-Communist regime.

The uprising began on August 1. The Poles established enclaves across the city, but failed to capture certain key points. They lacked weapons and equipment, but they had expected to be relieved in ten days by Soviet forces. The uprising dragged on until October 1. The increasingly desperate insurgents fought back with great determination against the German reinforcements.

Hitler ordered the total destruction of the city. In the end, almost 80 percent of Warsaw was razed. Some 15,000 members of the Home Army and 200,000 civilians were killed. The Germans suffered 17,000 casualties, but they held the city until February 1945.

After the failure of the uprising, many wondered why Stalin decided to halt his forces at the city gates and to block attempts by western Allies to air-drop supplies. Some claimed exhaustion of the Red Army. However, most likely, Stalin wanted to create a client regime in Poland after the war. The destruction of the Polish Home Army effectively destroyed those nationalists opposed to his plans.

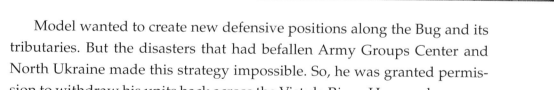

Model wanted to create new defensive positions along the Bug and its tributaries. But the disasters that had befallen Army Groups Center and North Ukraine made this strategy impossible. So, he was granted permission to withdraw his units back across the Vistula River. He was also promised reinforcements from Army Group South Ukraine. Before they could arrive, hopes of stopping the Red Army along the Vistula evaporated.

Marshal Konstantin Rokossovsky's 1st Belorussian Front drove the 120 miles (193 km) from Brest-Litovsk to the suburbs of Warsaw in just three days, between July 28 and 31. Crossing the Vistula to the south of the Polish capital at several points, Konev's men were similarly successful. During the latter part of the month they crossed the San River, a tributary of the Vistula. They evicted all of Army Group North Ukraine from southern Poland to hold the line along the Czechoslovakian border. The Germans abandoned the Polish oil wells that were vital to Germany's war effort.

> *The scale of the Red Army's victory between June and August was staggering.*

The scale of the Red Army's victory between June and August was staggering. In the northern and southern sectors of the eastern front the Soviets had pushed the Germans back 200 miles (320 km). The greatest advance was made in the center, where the front line now lapped around the suburbs of Warsaw, 400 miles (640 km) away from the positions at the start of the offensive. The liberation of the Baltic States and eastern Poland cost the Germans 920,000 men. Aside from these high casualty rates, Operation Bagration also brought the Red Army within a few hundred miles of Berlin. Hitler no longer had a buffer in the east to prevent an invasion of Nazi Germany.

By the end of August, the Red Army was in the outskirts of Warsaw. In expectation of Allied aid, Warsaw's resistance, the Polish Home Army, rose against the Germans in fierce street fighting. The Red Army proved reluctant to intervene, and the Poles were defeated.

Operation Bagration was drawing to an end while the Home Army was fighting for survival. Still, Soviet forces initiated a new offensive in the south, supposedly to liberate southeast Europe. However the offensive had a political motive—to pave the way for Soviet satellite states after the war. The attacks opened on August 20, and involved the 2nd and 3rd Ukrainian fronts, which cut through Army Group South Ukraine.

The German collapse left Hitler's occupied states in the region unable to fight on. First to surrender was Romania on August 23. Two days later its monarch, King Michael, signaled his country's withdrawal from the Axis and declared war on Germany. Bulgaria followed in early September. Never formally at war with the Soviet Union, Bulgaria and its leadership sought an armistice on September 9.

Stalin's next target was Hungary to prevent this wavering ally from exiting the Axis. The previous March, German forces had occupied the country. Its regent, Admiral Miklos Horthy, was forced to govern a more pro-Nazi government, which was very unpopular. The new government

HEINZ LANDAU

In 1944 Heinz Landau was a second lieutenant fighting with the Waffen SS in eastern Hungary. He was trying to stop the Red Army's assaults. He later remembered his poor physical state and the overwhelming odds he and his comrades faced.

Every square foot of ground was fought over desperately. We made a desperate stand at Tisza-Füred to allow for the crossing over the Tisza River of troops, as well as an ever-increasing flow of refugees. Just outside Tisza-Füred, having knocked out a large number of T-34s, we got involved in hand-to-hand fighting.

This was now tantamount to suicide, as the odds were against us. Here we were outnumbered by ten or fifteen to one. Russian morale was now at its highest, while ours was at its lowest. The Russians were now a well-fed lot, while we were a sorry-looking lot of flea-bitten skeletal scarecrows. My weight was down to 171 lb [under 9 stone 5 lb], and we were wheezing and tottering on our feet. Nevertheless, the spirit was still there and we considered ourselves far superior to the Ivans [nickname for the Soviet troops].

Extract from *The War Years 1939–1945: Eyewitness Accounts*, 1944.

sent Hungarian troops to the front and the country's Jewish community to death camps. Horthy dismissed the government on August 29 and began secret negotiations with the Soviet Union. On October 14 a news broadcast announced an armistice agreement with the Soviet Union. The Germans reacted quickly and seized Budapest, the capital. They established a new pro-Nazi regime.

> *Hungary remained a battlefield, and Budapest was placed under siege in late December.*

Hungary remained a battlefield, and Budapest was placed under siege in late December. This prompt action enabled what was left of Army Group South Ukraine (renamed Army Group South) to stabilize its positions in Hungary. German troops in the Balkans joined with Army Group North Ukraine (renamed Army Group A) in southern Poland. They created a weak but continuous front line against the Red Army. Just how poor the German positions were on the eastern front became clear in early 1945.

▶B-24 bombers were suitable for long-range, over-the-water missions. In 1944 the Allies began strategic air attacks on German factories and aircraft plants. Later, the B-24s bombed oil installations and transport systems.

6 The European Air War, 1944 to 1945

KEY PEOPLE	KEY PLACES
General Dwight D. Eisenhower	Schweinfurt, Germany
General Carl A. Spaatz	Regensburg, Germany
	Augsburg, Germany
	Nuremberg, Germany

In early 1944 the United States set up a new structure for conducting strategic bombing in Europe. The new U.S. Strategic Air Forces were led by General Carl A. Spaatz. In England, Lieutenant General James H. Doolittle took over the Eighth Air Force. The Fifteenth Air Force in Italy was commanded by Major General Nathan F. Twining. These two forces, with 1,000 heavy bombers, were to carry out Operation Argument— the destruction of the German aircraft industry, especially factories producing fighter planes.

The task was difficult. The Luftwaffe's fighter strength had increased. Fewer escorts were available for the Allied bombers. Only one fighter group was available in the European theater in early 1944. A large number of bombers were lost early in the year. Still, on February 20, 1944, the Eighth Air Force launched a great strategic air attack against aircraft factories in central Germany. An armada of 941 bombers and 700 fighters was launched. All the target factories were hit. Just twenty-one planes failed to return.

Big Week

For ten days of nonstop air attacks, known as Big Week, the Allies pounded German sites. On the night of February 20, the RAF sent 600 bombers to attack Stuttgart, another center of aircraft production. The next morning, bombers of the Eighth Air Force began to attack the aircraft factories at Brunswick. On February 22, B-17s and B-24s from the Fifteenth Air Force struck the Messerschmitt factory at Regensburg. The bombers of the Eighth Air Force at the same time hit factories in central Germany.

The mission was dogged by bad luck from the start. The Eighth Air Force's English bases were covered by dense clouds. Several bombers collided as they climbed up through them. Two divisions had to return to their airfields. Only the 1st Division continued. By this time German coastal radar had alerted the Luftwaffe to the invasion.

Out of the original ninety-nine bombers, only forty-four reached their targets.

The bombers had few escorts. As they crossed the German frontier, over one hundred German fighters attacked, completely surprising the Allies. By the time the bombers reached the Harz Mountains, forty-four lay scattered over the land below. Out of the original ninety-nine bombers, only forty-four reached their targets. Just two of these were undamaged. In the south the Fifteenth Air Force units successfully attacked the Messerschmitt factory. However, they were opposed by German 7th Air Division fighters and lost fourteen Allied bombers.

Bad weather halted the operations for twenty-four hours. Then, on February 24, 600 heavy bombers again set out. The Fifteenth Air Force's target was the Daimler-Benz airplane engine factory in eastern Austria. Once again they were strongly opposed. Of eighty-seven bombers, seventeen failed to return, with all ten bombers at the rear of the formation destroyed. Meanwhile, 477 Eighth Air Force bombers attacked the cities of Schweinfurt and Gotha, losing forty-four bombers. In a third wave, Eighth Air Force struck at Tutow, Kreising, and Posen.

On February 25, with good weather all over Germany, the Strategic Air Forces launched over 800 bombers to hit the Messerschmitt factories

Allied air raids at the Schweinfurt ball bearing plants in February 1944 caused much damage. During the war, the city of Schweinfurt was attacked a total of eight times by the U.S. Air Force and twice by the British Royal Air Force. Each successive raid caused more damage than the previous one.

at Regensburg and Augsburg from south and west. With no fighter escort, thirty-three of the Fortress bombers were shot down by German 7th Air Division planes. The bomber stream from the west, on the other hand, was larger and well escorted. Few German fighters managed to break through. Overall, the day's operations lost sixty-four heavy bombers. But the damage they inflicted on the aircraft factories was significant.

Big Week seemed at first to have been a success. At Regensburg the Messerschmitt factory appeared to be a wasteland. The German Air Ministry was about to build a new factory at a different site when it discovered that much of the Regensburg factory's machinery was repairable. By the beginning of June the factory was back to its former output. The

STRATEGY & TACTICS

STRATEGIC BOMBING: AN ASSESSMENT

The effectiveness of Allied bombing campaigns of World War II has been hotly debated. Undoubtedly, the bombing of Germany's aircraft production facilities caused massive disruption. However, it did not prevent a substantial rise in Luftwaffe fighter production from July 1943 to March 1945. The Germans maintained a monthly production figure of between 1,200 and 1,700 aircraft. Peak production reached 2,325 aircraft in 1944. However, without the sustained bombing campaign, the Germans would have reached their anticipated production level of about 3,000 aircraft per month in 1944, rising to 4,500 at the beginning of 1945.

While the German production of aircraft continued, operational units were not able to access fuel. Strategic bombing attacks on oil production prohibited access as did the bombing and interruption of the German transportation systems.

British air leaders, like Air Chief Marshal Arthur Harris, commander in chief of RAF Bomber Command, were disappointed that sustained bombing did not appear to affect civilian morale. As Luftwaffe historian Dr. Horst Boog pointed out long afterward, however, the morale was affected. In a paper delivered to the Royal Air Force Historical Society, Dr. Boog wrote:

"If the morale of the civilian population is defined as their will to continue to work for the war effort, then German morale was not broken. But it was certainly weakened, as recent studies have revealed, especially in cities suffering heavy attacks. People continued to do their duty in a fatalistic and apathetic mood, and this did not increase their devotion to the political cause and to productivity. It was not morale in this sense that kept them on the ball. Rather it was the desire to survive—which, under the circumstances of the political surveillance system, also meant doing what one was told and not shrinking in the presence of others—and the hope that one day their dreadful existence and experience would be over."

A B-24 bomber from the 15th Air Force releases its bombs over the rail yards of Muhldorf, Germany.

Messerschmitt factory at Augsburg needed only two weeks before production was back to normal. Albert Speer, the minister of munitions and war production, told other factories to move to different locations, making it more difficult for the Allies to attempt another knockout blow.

The raids were costly to the Luftwaffe. In the daylight offensive from January to April, 1944 the Lutfwaffe lost more than 1,000 pilots, with many of them being experienced veterans. Every time the Allies mounted a major raid, the Luftwaffe lost an average of fifty fighter pilots.

On March 6 and 8, 1944, Mustang fighter escorts took part in bitterly contested air battles over Berlin. The Allies lost over one hundred bombers but destroyed several key factories. The Germans lost eighty aircraft, or almost half of their defending force. By March 22, when 669 Allied bombers struck Berlin again, they met almost no opposition.

This map shows the major Allied bombing targets in Germany and Nazi-occupied Europe, 1944 to 1945.

Bomber Command Losses

Meanwhile, the RAF's night bombers suffered defensive attacks by the Luftwaffe's night fighters. In the course of three big air battles over Germany, Bomber Command endured crippling losses. One such night was March 30, 1944, when 795 heavy bombers left their English bases to attack the industrial center of Nuremberg. German night fighters retaliated from all over Germany, as one heavy Allied bomber after another fell burning from the sky. Some German pilots shot down multiple bombers, such as Oberleutnant Martin Becker, who destroyed six bombers in thirty minutes and shot down a seventh bomber after landing to refuel. For Bomber Command, the cost of the Nuremberg raid was horrendous. They lost ninety-five bombers that failed to return, and seventy-one were damaged. The loss of nearly 12 percent was the highest ever registered by Bomber Command. The defense of Nuremburg was the greatest victory by the German night fighters of the war. It was also its last.

The German Messerschmitt Nazi bombers, marked with a swastika, carried four crew members. They were equipped with two fluid-cooled motors and were armed with several light and heavy machine guns.

NORTH AMERICAN P-51 MUSTANG

The P-51 Mustang destroyed 4,950 enemy aircraft, more than any other fighter plane in Europe.

The North American P-51 Mustang was initially produced to meet an RAF requirement for a fast, heavily armed fighter able fly above 20,000 feet (6,100 m). It became one of the most famous fighters of World War II. The prototype flew on October 26, 1940. The first of 320 production Mustang Is for the RAF flew on May 1, 1941. They were powered by the 1,100-hp Allison engine.

The first two USAAF Mustang variants, both improved for ground attack, were also fitted with Allison engines. When the Mustangs were fitted with 1,400-hp Packard-built Rolls-Royce Merlin 61 engines, they showed great improvement in performance. Their maximum speed increased from 390 mph (627 km/h) to 441 mph (710 km/h).

Production of the Merlin-powered P-51B began in the fall of 1942. The factory at Inglewood, California, built 1,988 P-51Bs. The new plant at Dallas, Texas, built 1,750 aircraft designated as P-51C. In the first operational air escort mission, the 354th Fighter Group flew the P-51Bs from England in December 1943.

The most prolific Mustang was the P-51D, with a one-piece sliding cockpit canopy. The first model arrived in England in the late spring of 1944. They soon became the standard equipment of the USAAF Eighth Fighter Command. Armament included six .50-in. (12.7-mm) machine guns in the wings, plus provision for up to two 1,000-lb. (454-kg) bombs or six 5-in. (12.7-cm) rockets.

At last, the Allies had a fighter that could escort bombers all the way to Berlin and back, engaging enemy fighters before they could attack the bombers as they approached the targets. The fighters could dive down to strafe objectives on the homeward run. Without a doubt, the Mustang turned the tide of the air war over Europe.

Air Support Over Western Europe

The supreme commander of the Allied Expeditionary Force, General Dwight D. Eisenhower, took over strategic bombing operations in the European theater on April 14, 1944. One month later, the emphasis on strategic bombing switched from attacks on the enemy aircraft industry to oil installations and transportation systems.

During the last two weeks of May 1944 the Allies carried out heavy attacks on enemy coastal radar installations. The Germans had come to depend on coastal radar to warn of enemy approaches. However, by early June 1944, Allied air attacks destroyed about 80 percent of Germany's coastal radar capability.

On the night of June 5, 1944, RAF Bomber Command carried out operations to support the Allied landings in Normandy. Operations included attacks on heavy coastal gun batteries, radio countermeasures, and the simulation of airborne landings by dropping dummy paratroops. In Operation Taxtable, Lancasters and Stirlings dropped "Window" (bundles of radar-reflective metal strips) at four-second intervals to simulate the approach of an invasions fleet between Le Havre and Boulogne. In the twenty-four-hour period following the D-Day landings, the Allied air forces flew 14,674 sorties, losing just 113 aircraft. Combat air patrol (CAP) flew sorties over the invasion fleet and armed reconnaissance flew sorties inland. Throughout the day enemy communications came under heavy attack from medium bombers. Luftwaffe reaction on that first day was spotty.

During the last two weeks of May 1944 the Allies carried out heavy attacks on enemy coastal radar installations.

Although most support for the Allied armies came from the Tactical Air Forces, strategic bombers were still called in. On July 7, 1944, for example, 457 aircraft of RAF Bomber Command dropped 2,363 tons (2,143 tonnes) of bombs on targets north of Caen. Then on July 18, 1,570 heavy bombers dropped 7,700 tons (6,984 tonnes) on Caen itself. Four more major attacks took place up to mid-August.

The devastating effect of tactical air power was demonstrated on

August 17, 1944, when the remainder of sixteen German divisions were trapped in a 25-mile (40-km) corridor between Mortain and Falaise.

Three days of bombing by the Allied tactical air forces destroyed nearly all the heavy equipment belonging to the Germans. German casualties in the Falaise pocket were 10,000 killed, with 50,000 more taken prisoner.

On September 17, 1944, the Allies launched Operation Market Garden, the airborne invasion of Holland. It was part of a plan to position the British Second Army for a major offensive into the German industrial heartland.

The operation was only a partial success. The U.S. 82nd and 101st Airborne Divisions captured their objectives. However, the failure of the 1st British Airborne Division's operation at Arnhem, and the slow advance of XXX Corps, resulted in a disaster. Of the 10,000 British and Polish troops dropped at Arnhem, only 2,000 escaped. During the nine days of the operation, the USAAF and RAF together lost 238 aircraft and 139 gliders.

JIM ROSSER

In the closing months of World War II Germany had two operational jet aircraft types, with a third on the way. The Messerschmitt Me 262 and the Arado Ar 234 were in use. Flight Lieutenant Jim Rosser, flying a Spitfire XIV with No. 66 Squadron RAF, described an encounter with an Me 262 in September 1944.

I don't think anyone had actually managed to shoot down a 262 at that time, and I thought this was my big chance. I went down after him, flat out, but he saw me coming and opened the taps. Smoke trails streamed from his turbines and off he went; I hadn't a hope of catching him, so I gave up and rejoined the formation.

The incident had an interesting sequel. Years after the war, when I was stationed in Germany, I met a colonel in the Federal German Luftwaffe. We had a few drinks and got talking, and it turned out that he had flown 262s. We compared dates, places and times, and by one of those extraordinary coincidences it seems that he had almost certainly been the pilot of "my" 262. He said that if I had kept after him, I would probably have got him. His fuel was very low, and he couldn't have maintained full throttle for more than half a minute. But there it was; I got shot down near Arnhem a few days later, so I never did get another chance to have a crack at a jet.

Extract from *Fighter! The Story of Air Combat 1936–1945*, Robert Jackson, St. Martin's Press, New York, 1980.

German Countermeasures

Meanwhile, the Battle of Germany continued. As 1944 entered its second half, Allied strategic bombing forces were faced with new tactics and technology.

First there was the heavy flak. By mid-1944 it was radar-directed. The larger-caliber guns had a maximum ceiling of 35,000 feet (10,675 m). A few months later, in early 1945, some Luftwaffe flak units produced an antiaircraft rocket called Taifun, which could reach a ceiling of nearly 50,000 feet (15,245 m). At least one photograph exists showing one of these missiles just missing a B-17. The Germans also produced dangerous new fighters.

The greatest threat to Allied bomber formations was the German Me 262 jet fighter.

The greatest threat to Allied bomber formations was the German Me 262 jet fighter. It was heavily armed with four 30-mm cannons and, later, air-to-air rockets. The Eighth Air Force took the high-speed Me 262 very seriously and increased the size of fighter escorts so that every pair of bombers had a Mustang escort assigned to it. Meanwhile, attacks on jet-fighter bases were intensified. Many were rendered unusable.

On December 16, 1944, German forces launched a surprise attack through the Ardennes under cover of snow and fog.The Allied air forces could not react for several days. On December 24, in clearing weather, the U.S. Eighth Air Force sent 2,046 heavy bombers, escorted by 853 fighters, to support the Allied forces—the largest air strike of World War II.

At dawn on New Year's Day, 1945, the Luftwaffe launched Operation Bodenplatte (Baseplate). The enormous attack on Allied airfields in Belgium, Holland, and northern France used 800 fighter-bombers and was a complete surprise. The losses included 300 Allied aircraft and a comparable number of German aircraft. About 200 Luftwaffe aircraft were shot down by their own flak. Among the dead German pilots were fifty-nine experienced fighter leaders. The Luftwaffe never recovered.

Not until late January 1945 did the strategic offensive fully resume. In March, the Eighth Air Force felt the full impact of enemy jet fighters, when 1,250 American heavy bombers set out for Berlin to deliver the heaviest

Destruction similar to this happened all over Nazi-occupied territory through 1944 and early 1945. The bombings crippled the Nazi war machine.

attack of the war. A few miles short of the target they were attacked by thirty-seven Me 262s, which shot down nineteen bombers. On April 4 the German jets repeated their success when forty-nine Me 262s attacked 150 B-17s over Nordhausen, destroying fifteen of them. Four days later this same jet-fighter unit destroyed twenty-eight Allied bombers over northern and central Germany. In return, Allied fighters destroyed 133 Me 109s and Fw 190s. No matter how successful the German jets were, they scored too few victories, too late. The Allies remained in firm control of the air.

On April 25, B-17s of the 384th Bomb Group returned to their base in Northamptonshire, England, after completing a bombing mission to support U.S. forces east of the Rhine. That night, ninety RAF bombers attacked an oil refinery in southern Norway. These were the last times Allied heavy bombers would be used in the European War.

▶German sailors aboard a U-boat surrender to forces of the U. S. Navy in the final year of the Battle of the Atlantic. Superior Allied tactical and technological strategies finally overcame attacks from the feared German U-boats.

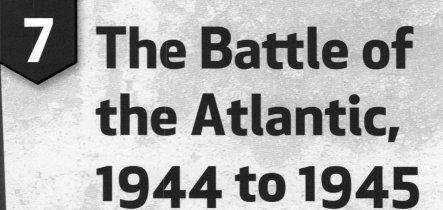

7

The Battle of the Atlantic, 1944 to 1945

KEY PEOPLE	KEY PLACES
⚑ Admiral Karl Dönitz	Atlantic Ocean

In mid-1943 Germany's war machine was desperate. Admiral Karl Dönitz, in May of that year, ordered U-boats to abandon attacks on North Atlantic convoy routes. He did not intend to end the U-boat campaign. Dönitz knew his boats were outclassed and outnumbered by the Allied forces, and he decided that the U-boats had to stay on the offensive. Germany's war situation was becoming so desperate that the U-boats must continue to attack, no matter the high rate of casualties. To make things better for his men, he would find new locations and tactics for the U-boats and make improvements to them. Despite his efforts, Dönitz and his U-boats would never regain the initiative.

The Search for a New Strategy

Dönitz's first move was to send part of his force to the Azores Islands, near the Bay of Biscay, to attack convoys heading from the United States to Gibraltar and the Mediterranean. However, U.S. escort groups sank many U-boats in the area, including several U-tankers, or fuel-carrying submarines. During the summer of 1943 the Allies sunk many U-boats crossing the Bay of Biscay because German instruments could not detect the radar signals from Allied aircraft. U-boats on the surface were often taken by surprise. Dönitz ordered the U-boat fleet to fight off attacks using their antiaircraft guns and to avoid diving. However, in June and July of 1943, Allied air attacks sank more than forty U-boats. For the rest of the war U-boats in the area stayed submerged as long as possible.

In early 1944 the Allies sank two U-boats carrying technicians who were studying how Allied transmissions worked.

Allied attacks in the area were strengthened by support groups of antisubmarine ships, which had no escort duties. If a support group found a U-boat, it stayed with it until the U-boat was destroyed. In early 1944 the Allies sank two U-boats carrying technicians who were studying how Allied transmissions worked. Upon interrogation, the survivors provided the Allies with valuable information.

The snorkel was another German technical failure. A Dutch invention, it fell into the hands of the Germans in 1940. Because of testing, the first snorkel boat, *U-264*, did not patrol until early 1944. It was promptly destroyed by the British 2nd Support Group. Snorkels did not go into general U-boat service until after D-Day.

In September 1943 the U-boats began using acoustic torpedoes to strike at the escort ships. However, a U-boat firing an acoustic torpedo had to dive deep immediately or else the torpedo could turn and attack the U-boat. Thus the U-boat crew could not assess the results of their attack. Many torpedoes exploded prematurely, and others were decoyed off course by the Allies. In the first battle using acoustic torpedoes, the U-boats sank three escorts and six merchant ships. In May 1944, *U-549* sank the escort carrier USS *Block Island*, the last major Allied ship sunk by U-boats.

IMPROVING U-BOATS

This German U-boat has fired a missile against an Allied convoy. The Germans and Allies introduced countermeasures against each other to improve their technological advantages in the Battle of the Atlantic.

As well as creating new types of submarines, German engineers and scientists also improved existing U-boats in the later years of the war. The first improvement was the *Schnorchel*, a ventilation pipe that worked like a swimmer's snorkel. (U.S. servicemen took the English word from the German.) World War II submarines used diesel engines and electric motors when submerged. Because their batteries needed recharging, the electric motors had limited power and speed. With the snorkel, the submarine could remain submerged with the diesels running. The snorkel head was so small that it was unlikely to show on radar. The first snorkel U-boats went into action at the start of 1944. The device made them harder to catch. But at the same time a submerged U-boat was less likely to find targets of its own.

The first new type of torpedo was introduced in early 1943. It followed a zigzag course after launch. It weaved in front of a convoy and, if it failed to hit one of the leading ships, would try to strike one following behind. The second type of torpedo had an acoustic device designed to home in on the noise made by a nearby escort ship. First used in September 1943, these torpedoes were successful. But the Allies developed countermeasures to lead the torpedoes off-target or make them explode. They also produced their own acoustic torpedoes.

Radar and other electronic technology helped Allies' success in late 1943. Because Germany lacked coordinated research and development, Dönitz finally set up a single body to handle all naval scientific research.

By February 1944 most U-tankers had been sunk. Allied air cover extended to more distant waters. Dönitz sent his boats back into the waters off the British Isles. This was the first time since 1940 that this area had been the focus of attacks. In response, the British sent in escort carriers and support groups. In the first three months of 1944 they destroyed another thirty-six U-boats. In the same period more than 3,000 merchant ships passed through in convoy. Only three were sunk. By March, Dönitz knew that his fleet was in trouble. He gave orders that U-boats were to give up any attempt to fight in packs. Instead they were to operate singly. It was yet another sign of how much the Allied forces were in control.

Between September 1943 and May 1944, the number of U-boats sunk by Allies was more than the number of Allied merchant ships sunk by German U-boats.

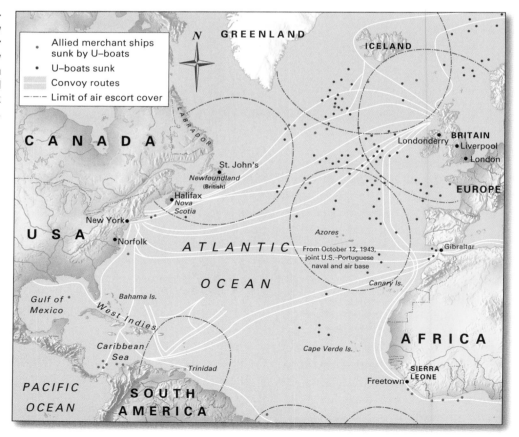

The German battleship *Tirpitz* lies at anchor in the Alta Fjord in northern Norway. The ship is protected by anti-torpedo nets. The battleship saw service from 1941 to 1944, when RAF bombers sank her.

Sinking the *Tirpitz*

The battleship *Tirpitz* had been badly damaged in a daring midget submarine attack in September 1943. However, British commanders wanted to make sure the ship would never again threaten convoys. By April 1944 British code breakers knew that *Tirpitz* was at its base in Norway and had been repaired. On April 3 an aircraft-carrier force attacked the ship, putting it out of action for another few months. Further carrier attacks in May failed. In September RAF planes attacked *Tirpitz* with massive bombs. Another RAF attack in November 1944 sunk her, trapping in the upturned hull 1,000 men out of her 2,500 member crew.

Tirpitz had ironically never fired its main armament against another ship. Yet its very presence had caused problems for the Arctic convoys taking supplies to Russia. However, even before *Tirpitz* was sunk, those convoys, with massive escort forces, had begun to get through with far fewer losses. For example, in the spring of 1944, convoy JW.58 of forty-eight ships from Iceland to Murmansk was protected by two escort carriers and thirty antisubmarine vessels. The convoy lost no ships in the attack.

LIBERTY SHIPS

TECH

Liberty ships helped the Allies win the Battle of the Atlantic. The Liberty ships originated from an old British design for a mass-produced cargo ship. The design was taken to the United States in 1940 and entered production.

American shipbuilding was put under the control of men like Henry Kaiser, a brilliant engineer and organizer. He applied assembly line techniques similar to those used by the auto industry. He used a work force with little previous experience in heavy engineering. Many of his workers were women, who were now doing "a man's job." Such workers were celebrated in the character of "Rosie the Riveter." However, the ships were not riveted but welded—one reason that they could be built so quickly. The first Liberty ship took about six months to build. By the middle of 1942 building Liberty ships took less than half that time. As a publicity stunt, a Liberty ship was built in less than a week.

The Liberty ships carried about 11,000 tons (9,977 tonnes) of cargo each at a speed of about 11 knots (20 km/h). They were fairly large and fast by the standards of the time. More than 2,700 were built in all, and they were produced in the later stages of the war at the rate of three a day. The goods carried by ships like these were the foundation for the Allied victories of 1943 to 1945.

Overlord and the U-boats

Allied dominance over the U-boats and the huge output from American shipyards were the basis for Allied strategy in 1944 to 1945. The U.S. Army and U.S. Army Air Force could be deployed wherever the Allied leaders chose—to the Mediterranean or to readying for the D-Day invasion. Hundreds of thousands of American personnel and their weapons and equipment would cross the Atlantic. Thanks to the Allied navies, almost all would do so safely.

The American soldiers transported to the European war zone sailed in troopships converted from luxury passenger liners. The largest ships, like the British *Queen Elizabeth*, could carry up to 15,000 soldiers. Sinking such a target would have been a great achievement for a U-boat commander. The luxury liners did not sail in convoys but operated independently, without escorts. The liners were very fast and were given carefully selected routes that evaded the enemy.

Allied superiority over German U-boats had additional results. The climate in western Europe is influenced by weather systems that develop over the Atlantic. With few U-boats remaining in the Atlantic, German forecasters did not get much weather information. They could not predict the break in the weather on June 6, D-Day. Rommel had gone home to visit his wife. Other German units were also taken by surprise. The German lack of preparedness was an unexpected bonus for the Allied leaders.

Although he had no reliable information about the time or location, Admiral Karl Dönitz was convinced that an invasion, like D-Day, would take place. He thus assembled a strike force of about forty U-boats at French bases. Actually caught by surprise, none were at their stations on June 6. Although they hurried into action, they ran into the massive Allied anti-submarine forces. The U-boats that had not yet been fitted with snorkels were almost all either sunk or badly damaged. Those with snorkels were only a bit more successful. As many as twenty U-boats were sunk in the English Channel area over the following two months.

In addition to U-boats, the Germans had also built midget submarines that were successful later in the war off Normandy and in the Thames and Scheldt estuaries. Pressure sensitive mines were another hazard for Allied shipping. The Germans used them to block French and Belgian ports that the Allies had captured and wished to bring back into service.

"Marder" type human torpedoes were one of the more unusual German inventions of 1944. They were not suicide weapons. Yet their crude design allowed only two out of three mariners to return safely after launch of the torpedo.

Loss of the Atlantic Ports

On August 16, 1944, Dönitz ordered his U-boats to abandon their French bases. They were being cut off and surrounded by advancing Allied forces. The capture of these ports in 1940 had helped the Germans develop their U-boat campaign. Now the ports were useless.

Allied successes on land were matched by superiority in the skies over Europe. At last the strategic bomber forces began to live up to the boasts their leaders had made years before: that their attacks could damage the German submarine force. Direct attacks on U-boats were now effective. The bombers also hit transportation networks and manufacturing plants. New German "electro-U-boats" were being built in sections at inland factories. Since each U-boat section weighed one hundred tons, they were transported by water to the coast for final assembly. In September RAF Bomber Command attacked the Dortmund–Ems waterway canal, draining it and others and keeping them out of service for U-boat transport. In addition, coastal shipyards were attacked. Mine-laying attacks over the Baltic and the advance of Soviet armies made the previously safe U-boat training areas increasingly dangerous and restricted.

Final Coastal Operations.

Early in 1945 the U-boat fleet was still strong. There were 166 operational boats and 278 still in training as late as April. The U-boats operated in the relatively shallow waters close to the British coast. Here U-boats could hide on the bottom among the wrecks that littered the area.

The Allies could not track the U-boats very well. Allied aircraft radar was useless, since the U-boats spent most of the time underwater using their snorkels. A submerged U-boat could not transmit radio messages, so Allied code breaking and radio detection did not help, either. The U-boats accomplished little during this time. Their periscopes gave them limited views. During snorkeling operations, their engines drowned out any sound-detection equipment. The U-boats were essentially blind and deaf.

The U-boat crews suffered horribly. A boat might stay submerged for several weeks without proper ventilation. The stench of rotting food and human waste combined with high levels of carbon monoxide. Sudden

"NEW U-BOATS"

TECH

The German submarines of 1939 to 1943 were not much different from those used in World War I. They could not remain submerged for very long, even though they needed to avoid radar detection. When the subs were underwater, they were too slow. Improvements like snorkels, better radar-warning devices, and new torpedoes did not really help. Eventually, German scientists modernized the design of conventional submarines, a solution which worked. They also developed an entirely new technology, a solution which failed.

Like earlier U-boats, the modernized designs had both diesel engines and battery-powered electric motors. They also featured streamlined hulls and bigger, more powerful batteries, which gave much higher underwater speed and greater endurance.

In the later months of the war older U-boats were doomed if detected by escort ships. The new "electro-U-boats" were faster when submerged than many of the Allied escorts. Two types were made: the smaller and shorter-range Type XXIII and the larger Type XXI. The problem for Germany in 1944 to 1945 was producing them and getting them into service.

The new-technology U-boats were even more radical. They used a chemical system, invented by German scientist Helmuth Walter, to generate oxygen so that their diesel engines could be run underwater without any air intake. Faster underwater than on the surface, the system could not be made to work reliably. Not one "Walter boat" ever saw war service. Once again, poor planning and Hitler's obsession with wonder weapons wasted Germany's resources.

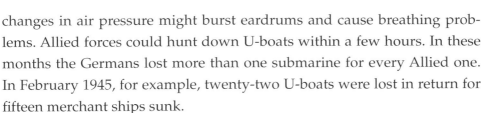

changes in air pressure might burst eardrums and cause breathing problems. Allied forces could hunt down U-boats within a few hours. In these months the Germans lost more than one submarine for every Allied one. In February 1945, for example, twenty-two U-boats were lost in return for fifteen merchant ships sunk.

In February, however, the first of the new Type XXIII electro-U-boats entered service. They were able to attack and then use their high underwater speed to escape sonar range. However, for the Germans, it was too little, too late. Just over sixty Type XXIIIs entered service. Only ten completed training and trials. The larger and stronger Type XXI U-boats were delayed in production. Though 120 were built, only two went to sea, the first on April 30. The electro-U-boats sank only five Allied ships, including the *Avondale Park* on May 7—one of the last U-boat victims of the war.

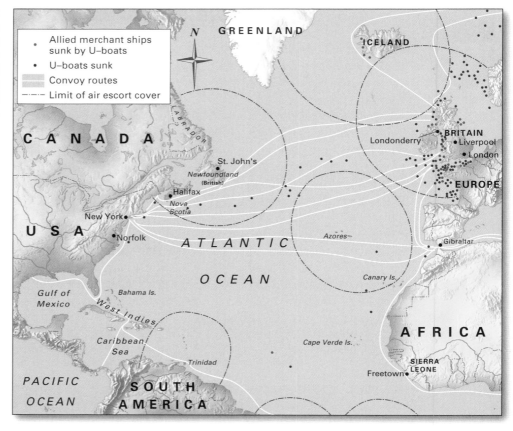

During the last stages of the Battle of the Atlantic, most of the German U-boat fleet occupied the waters off the coast of Britain and western Europe.

Map legend:
- Allied merchant ships sunk by U-boats
- U-boats sunk
- Convoy routes
- Limit of air escort cover

Surrender of the U-Boats

Dönitz's representatives surrendered to General Bernard Montgomery on May 4, 1945. The surrender covered all German naval forces. Of the surviving U-boats, more than 200 were scuttled. Two sailed to neutral Argentina rather than give in. More than 150 U-boats surrendered over the next few days. Some were captured in ports in Germany or Norway, but others surfaced in their operational areas to be escorted into captivity. The longest battle of the war was over.

A U.S. Coast Guard officer later wrote that more sailors were killed in the campaign than in all the naval battles of the previous 500 years. About 50,000 Allied merchant seamen died in the Atlantic, two-thirds of them British. Some 2,500 cargo ships were sunk. Merchant seamen were

Germany's Grand Admiral Karl Dönitz *(on left)* is escorted by a British army officer. Dönitz is being led away from his headquarters in Flensburg, Germany, after his arrest on May 24, 1945.

officially civilians. Roughly 20 percent of Britain's merchant seamen were killed in the war, a higher percentage than in any of the U. S. or British armed services. Almost 700 U-boats were sunk, and about 27,500 U-boat men were killed out of 39,000 who served. Like every other campaign of World War II, the Battle of the Atlantic saw incredible death, destruction, and suffering on an almost unimaginable scale.

▶Operation Plunder, the Allied crossing of the Rhine, was preceded by massive artillery bombardment. These British 5.5-inch guns fired continuously at German positions for fifteen hours before the crossing began.

8 From the Rhine to the Elbe

The Battle of the Bulge was a disaster for Hitler. His grand march toward Antwerp was repulsed by the Allies. The surviving units were under strength and short of weapons and equipment. The fuel shortage had reached the crisis point. It was clear to many of his generals that the German army could not continue fighting a two-front war.

Yet Hitler still demanded more. He moved crippled units as if they were fresh. He directed nonexistent forces to the battle-front. He dismissed the assessments of generals who were strong enough to point out Hitler's delusions. Hitler's belief in ultimate victory remained unshakeable.

Even though the Ardennes offensive was failing short of its objectives, Hitler wanted further action. The Allies were flooding reinforcements into the battle at the expense of weakening their forces to the north and south. The German Army Group G under General Johannes von Blaskowitz was ordered to take advantage of this situation. He attacked the U.S. Seventh Army, part of General Jacob Devers's Sixth Army Group, which was in position from the Swiss border to southern Luxembourg.

The operation was code-named *Nordwind* (Northwind). It opened on December 31, 1944. Blaskowitz hit the Seventh Army, which was under the command of General Alexander M. Patch. The plan was to join with German troops advancing north from near Colmar. Strasbourg, a French border city, was the ultimate goal. Patch's men fell back from their positions. Eisenhower thought of abandoning Strasbourg. But General Charles de Gaulle intervened. He insisted that the loss of the city would hurt French morale. Secretly, de Gaulle had ordered the French First Army to defend the city. However, Eisenhower agreed with de Gaulle, and Patch was ordered to defend the city at all costs.

Allied Advance to the Rhine

The Germans battered away at Devers's defenses for about two weeks. However, they failed to break the line. Devers ordered a counterstrike against the Colmar Pocket. It was launched on January 20 by the French First Army and several U.S. divisions. Despite their hopeless position, the Germans refused to surrender. They fought on until February 9. The offensive cost the French and American troops 20,000 casualties, but German losses were twice that. The failure of Nordwind and the loss of the Colmar Pocket was decisive. Devers's troops were now poised to strike into Germany itself.

The offensive cost the French and American troops 20,000 casualties, but German losses were twice that.

Devers's arrival on the west bank of the Rhine was matched by that of Allied generals Bernard Montgomery and Omar Bradley to the north. Montgomery's command, the 21st Army Group, was reinforced by the U.S. Ninth Army. The more northerly push, Operation Veritable, was to punch through an area of heavy forest, the Reichswald, on the Dutch-German border. The southern arm of the assault, code-named Grenade, was the responsibility of Lieutenant General William Simpson's U.S. Ninth Army. His troops were to cross the Roer River and then drive for the Rhine at Düsseldorf to link with Allied forces from the north.

Veritable opened on February 8, but the troops struggled to get through the Reichswald. Both good German defense and heavy rain slowed them down. By February 19 they were still bogged down just 15 miles (24 km) from their starting line.

Grenade, scheduled to open on February 10, was also delayed. It finally began on February 23. By nightfall four U.S. divisions had crossed the Roer and were striking out to the north and east. The defending Fifteenth Army was forced back, despite the arrival of German reinforcements. This breach in the line allowed Simpson's men to push north. On March 6 the two divisions met at Wesel on the west bank of the Rhine. What was left of the German Fifteenth Army retreated to the east bank. The 21st Army Group had taken 53,000 prisoners and now occupied the Rhine from Emmerich near the Dutch border to Düsseldorf—a distance of 60 miles (96 km).

The German forces had no respite. Bradley's 12th Army Group also pushed out on February 9. His First Army under General Courtney H. Hodges battered through the Hürtgen Forest and fanned out toward the Ahr River. The German line crumbled. The Allies took prisoners every day. The speed of the advance caught many German commanders by surprise.

In the following weeks, towns and cities on the Rhine fell to the Allies. The Allies, though, had not captured any intact bridges over the river. The advance seemed stalled along the Rhine. However, the German demolition of the bridges was not complete. On March 7 electrifying news reached Bradley's headquarters. U. S. troops had captured a bridge at Remagen, a little north of where the Ahr joins the Rhine. Troops had established positions on the east bank of the Rhine.

> *In the following weeks, towns and cities on the Rhine fell to the Allies.*

Patton was also striking out for the Rhine. He had punched from his positions along the Moselle River through the Eifel region. Continuous attacks pounded the German line. On March 7 his 4th Armored Division reached the Rhine. By late March the Rhineland campaign was over. In less than two months some 60,000 German soldiers were killed or wounded. The Allies captured 250,000 men at a cost of fewer than 20,000 casualties.

THE BRIDGE AT REMAGEN

The Ludendorff Bridge across the Rhine River at Remagen, captured by U. S. First Army on March 11, 1945.

The Allies hoped to capture an intact bridge over the Rhine to speed their drive into Germany during spring 1945. At Remagen the tantalizing opportunity presented itself.

The crossing at Remagen was actually called the Ludendorff Bridge. Discovered intact by an armored patrol from the U.S. First Army on March 7, 1945, it was primed for destruction. However, the blast had been delayed to aid the escape of German troops from the west bank of the river. An assault was speedily arranged under Sergeant Karl Timmermann, an American citizen of German descent. As the attack began, the Germans blew the explosive charges that were supposed to send the bridge crashing into the waters below. Even though damaged, the bridge remained intact. The surrender of the small force of defenders gave the American forces free passage to the east bank of the Rhine.

Over the following days four Allied divisions hurried over the bridge to establish an encampment on the east bank of the Rhine. Hitler, furious, ordered the execution of four officers who had been responsible for the bridge's defense. The Germans made numerous attempts to destroy the bridge by bomber crews, V-2 rocket units, and frogmen. All efforts failed. However, the sheer weight of Allied traffic caused its collapse. The bridge crashed into the Rhine on March 17, killing twenty-six U. S. personnel. Since Allied engineers had already constructed a pontoon bridge nearby, the collapse did not interrupt Allied strategy.

The Rhine Crossings

By spring 1945 the Allies were ready to cross the last natural barrier between them and the German homeland. Eisenhower made the choice of where to begin. He selected Montgomery's 21st Army Group to lead the way. Montgomery's troops lay opposite the flat terrain of northern Germany. The shortest route to Berlin was across the northern terrain. Both Bradley's command and Devers's 6th Army Group supported Montgomery's efforts. Montgomery's offensive was to be part of a broad-front attack on the Rhine. The Rhine crossing was scheduled for March 23. On the day before, Patton launched his own surprise attack across the river from near Oppenheim. He used no pre-assault bombardment to warn the Germans. Thanks to plenty of bridging equipment Patton supplied his army, his troops stormed ashore with few casualties. Within two days, four divisions had poured over the Rhine. By March 28, Patton's fast-moving armored columns had pushed about 100 miles (160 km) into Germany.

These African-American troops from the 784th Tank Battalion are battle-ready for driving their Sherman tanks across the Rhine River in March 1945.

Montgomery's offensive had two parts. The first was an amphibious assault across the Rhine known as Operation Plunder. The second was an airborne drop, code-named Varsity. The British general had twenty-seven divisions (thirteen American, twelve British, and two Canadian) and 3,000 artillery pieces. British and U. S. bombers had isolated the zone from the rest of Germany by smashing rail and road links into the area. Some 60,000 engineers were on hand to build pontoon bridges over the river. Landing craft and amphibious assault vehicles would transport the troops. Smoke-generating equipment masked the preparations. The opposing German First Parachute Army, consisting of seven exhausted divisions, awaited

This map shows the major Allied attacks into Germany and the Allied rendez-vous with the Soviet Red Army on the Elbe River, 1945.

Varsity. Other units were available, but these were held back to counter an expected airborne landing by Montgomery's Anglo–U.S. XVIII Airborne Corps. The Germans expected a repeat of Arnhem, but Montgomery had learned his lessons.

Plunder opened at 5:00 p.m. on March 23 with an artillery bombardment that lasted until 9:45 a.m. the next day. The British Second Army led the way by crossing around Wesel. German resistance was sporadic. Their efforts were further undermined by the 10:00 a.m. arrival of General Matthew Ridgway's 14,000 paratroopers. They landed just a few miles from Wesel. By nightfall Montgomery's troops held about 30 miles (48 km) of the east bank and pushed deeper into German territory. Within three days engineers built twelve bridges over the Rhine. Allied forces were pouring in great strength across the bridges.

The breaching of the Rhine was quickly followed by more bad news for the Germans. Other Allied armies had advanced further into the German homeland by the end of March. On March 25 the First Army, under General Courtney Hodges, broke out of the Remagen bridgehead. The First Army covered the 70 miles (112 km) to Marburg in two days. Farther south, General Jacob Devers's army group bridged the Rhine at two points. On March 26 the U.S. Seventh Army crossed around Mannheim. Five days later General de Lattre de Tassigny's French First Army crossed at Gersheim. These successes signaled the end of coordinated German efforts to defend the Rhine. German forces on the western front were weak, poorly equipped, and without fuel.

Eisenhower's Strategic Dilemma

The supreme Allied commander now faced a difficult choice. Should he concentrate his resources and drive toward Berlin? Or, should he continue the broad push by all three army groups to crush what remained of the German war machine? The second option had political considerations. Establishing a western Allied presence in Berlin before the arrival of the Red Army was a concern. The first option was influenced by a belief that the Nazis had a last-ditch defensive position called the National Redoubt in the southern German mountains of Bavaria.

Eisenhower selected the first, broader option. Despite the objections of British prime minister Winston Churchill and General Montgomery, Eisenhower's decision was supported by President Franklin D. Roosevelt and Army Chief of Staff George C. Marshall. Joseph Stalin also approved of Eisenhower's decision. The second option ensured that Red Army would have a free hand to capture Berlin and to avenge the horrors inflicted on the Soviet Union by the Germans in 1941.

Eisenhower's plan was to maintain a broad advance by his three army groups. The objective was to reach the line of the Elbe River, some 200 miles (320 km) east of the Rhine but 125 miles (200 km) short of Berlin. The bulk of Montgomery's forces were to push into northern Germany. Devers's command was to drive through Bavaria along the valley of the Danube River toward Czechoslovakia and Austria. They were also to guard the flanks of what was becoming the main Allied drive: Bradley's army group, moving through central Germany toward Leipzig on the Elbe. Before Bradley could head for Leipzig, he faced stiff German resistance in the Ruhr industrial region. According to Eisenhower's strategy, the Ruhr industrial district was the principal remaining target.

Bradley. . . faced stiff German resistance. . .

Encircling the Ruhr

The Ruhr valley, made up of industrial towns and cities on the east bank of the Rhine, was vulnerable to attack. The U.S. First Army and the Ninth Army faced Field Marshal Walther Model's Army Group B in battle. Model, a general of proven ability, now led a dispirited and poorly equipped force. The U.S. First Army broke out of the Remagen bridgehead on March 25, and the Ninth Army followed around Wesel on March 29. The First Army quickly cut through German opposition as it headed along the southern edge of the pocket. Then it turned north toward Lippstadt. Here, on April 1, the First and Ninth Armies united. Model was sealed off. A half-hearted relief attempt failed on April 4. That day Bradley's armies set about removing the pocket.

The fighting was intense for ten days. The Germans defended the area's towns and villages with great determination. Then their morale collapsed and they began to surrender by the thousands. Hitler at that point ordered Model to break out of the pocket, but he did not have the resources or will to do so. The Allied victory destroyed Model's Army Group B. The toll of prisoners reached 315,000 men—more than in any other battle of the war. Field Marshal Model could not face either his surrender to the Allies or the wrath of Hitler. He committed suicide shortly before his command was overwhelmed.

> *Field Marshal Model could not face either his surrender to the Allies or the wrath of Hitler.*

Final Pushes into Germany

Even as the Ruhr battle continued, the Allies were fanning out across Germany, making for the Elbe River. In a twist of fate, the Allies made great use of the Autobahn (freeway) system that Hitler had constructed for the German army in 1940. These highways reached into the heart of Nazi Germany. The Allied columns occasionally met resistance, but sometimes

WEREWOLVES AND THE NATIONAL REDOUBT

STRATEGY & TACTICS

If Berlin were captured and Hitler killed, the Werewolves were part of a plan to allow the Third Reich to fight on from a National Redoubt. (A redoubt is a secure place that can be easily defended.)

John Foster Dulles in September 1944 first described the idea that the Nazis had a National Redoubt. Dulles was the U.S. chief of intelligence gathering. He suggested that the Nazis would make a last stand around Berchtesgaden, Hitler's home in Bavaria. In 1945 Allied units were directed to seize the area. In fact, the idea of a National Redoubt did not even occur to Hitler until the end of April 1945. By then it was far too late.

The presence of Werewolves were also overestimated. They were believed to be many small cells of young, dedicated Nazis scattered across Germany. The cells were commanded from the National Redoubt. The Werewolves had supposedly been given orders to commit acts of sabotage and assassination in Allied-occupied Germany. They were, in reality, few in number, poorly organized, and badly equipped.

the opposing Germans took the opportunity to surrender. Many of the remaining enemy troops were members of the ill-equipped *Volkssturm* home defense force. They were eager to surrender as soon as possible. Driving through the countryside, Allied troops entered towns and villages draped in white surrender flags. They passed long lines of dejected German soldiers heading west to avoid capture by the Red Army.

In the north, Montgomery's army group drove into northern and eastern Holland, where much of the population was starving because of the lack of food distribution. Then Montgomery's army began to strike out across the north German plain toward the Baltic coast and Hamburg. The troops had to cross heavily defended rivers—the Ems, Weser, Aller, and finally the Elbe. They reached the Elbe on April 26. On May 2, the Allies reached Lübeck on the Baltic coast, the same day that Montgomery's forces also met the Red Army.

EYEWITNESS

MILTON SHULMAN

In the final days of their drive through Germany, Allied troops faced German *Volkssturm* (home defense) units. These were made up of men too old or too young for regular military service. These units were forced to fight with little training and equipment. Shulman, a major fighting with the Canadian First Army, interrogated a Volkssturm officer. He revealed his battalion's lack of preparedness.

I had 400 men in my battalion and we were ordered to go into line in our civilian clothes. I told the local party leader that I could not accept the responsibility of leading men into battle without uniforms [this broke the accepted rules of warfare; the Allies would have been acting within their rights to shoot such prisoners out of hand]. Just before commitment the unit was given 180 Danish rifles, but there was no ammunition. We also had four machine guns and 100 antitank Panzerfausts. None of the men had received any training in firing a machine gun, and they were all afraid of handling the antitank weapon. Although my men were quite ready to help their country, they refused to go into battle without uniforms and without training. What can a Volkssturm man do with a rifle without ammunition? The men went home. That was the only thing they could do.

Extract taken from *The History of World War II*, edited by Brigadier Peter Young, 1972.

As the Anglo–Canadian troops advanced, they uncovered, as did the U. S. troops to the south, evidence of Hitler's genocide of Europe's Jewish community. When the Bergen–Belsen extermination camp was overrun, troops found 10,000 unburied dead and mass graves filled with 40,000 corpses. About 39,000 inmates were still alive. They were in a pitiful condition—28,000 of them died over the next days.

In the center, Bradley's 12th Army Group pushed eastward from the Ruhr and crossed the Weser with little difficulty. Its First Army captured 70,000 German troops in the Harz Mountains between April 14 and 21. On April 25, in the village of Torgau on the Elbe, U. S. and Soviet troops met for the first time—a historic event. Patton's Third Army also advanced toward the Elbe. Its lead elements had reached the Mulda River, a tributary of

Its First Army captured 70,000 German troops in the Harz Mountains between April 14 and 21.

the Elbe, by the close of the war. Patton then led his men along the valley of the Danube into eastern Bavaria, crossing into western Czechoslovakia and northern Austria. On May 7 he was ordered to halt his forces just as they were preparing to liberate Prague, the Czech capital.

General Milton Halsey (center) and members of his 97th Infantry Division inspect the facilities at the Flossenburg concentration camp in April 1945. Allied troops across Germany were horrified and deeply moved at their discoveries of similar camps.

THE GERMAN SURRENDERS

Although Hitler was in charge of Germany, events had slipped from his control. He had demanded that Nazi Germany go down fighting, its people destroyed, towns and cities leveled for failing their leader. Events were very much different in the field, where senior commanders sensed the realities of the situations. Yet no one was willing to move until the very last moment, either out of loyalty to Hitler or fear of the consequences.

The turning point came in late April and early May. Hitler committed suicide on April 30. Berlin's garrison fell on May 2. Hitler's successor, Grand Admiral Karl Dönitz, immediately ordered his field commanders to end resistance. They would accept the Allied terms of unconditional surrender.

The first meeting took place at Lünenberg Heath on May 3 between British Field Marshal Montgomery and representatives of German forces in the north of the country. Since there was no representative of the Luftwaffe present, the British field marshal brought discussions to an end. The meeting continued the following day, this time with a Luftwaffe officer. A surrender document relating to north Germany and the Netherlands was signed.

The document to end the European War was signed at Reims, the headquarters of the Supreme Headquarters Allied Expeditionary Force, on May 7. Representatives from the main Allies were present, as were senior German officers. The document ordered hostilities to end at 11:01 p.m. on May 8. Early the following day the surrender process was completed by a ceremony in Berlin.

A few Allied soldiers supervise wounded German prisoners as they are being loaded into a U. S. Army transport plane.

These four members of the military police (M. P.) pause along a German road in May 1945. Their military newspapers, the *Stars and Stripes*, have the headlines that Nazi Germany has surrendered.

Devers's 6th Army Group moved though western and central Bavaria to ensure that no Germans could retreat to the alleged National Redoubt. The route took his troops through some important sites linked to the rise of Hitler and the Nazis. A short, vicious battle to capture Nuremberg, site of Nazi rallies in the past, ensued. This was followed on April 19 by the capture of Munich, the spiritual home of Nazism. At Munich, Hitler had attempted to seize power in 1923. The final prize was Berchtesgaden, Hitler's summer residence. It fell to the French 2nd Armored Division on May 4. Like much of the Third Reich, Berchtesgaden was in ruins after a recent Allied bombing. Also on May 4 at the Brenner Pass, Allied forces pushing south through Bavaria met Allied forces pushing north through Italy—another historic meeting.

Various discussions and local surrenders took place in the final days of the European war. Adolf Hitler committed suicide on April 30, 1945. However, the formal surrender of the Third Reich and the end of the war in Europe came on May 8. The Nazi State outlived its creator by little more than a week.

Timeline

1939 • Germany invades Poland.
- Britain, France, Australia, and New Zealand declare war on Germany.
- Denmark signs nonaggression treaty with Nazi Germany.
- South Africa and Canada declare war on Germany.

1940 • Germany overruns Denmark.
- Spain adopts "nonbelligerency."
- Franco signs Anti-Comintern Pact with Germany, Italy, and Japan.
- Irish Free State (southern Ireland) remains neutral.

1941 • Dublin attacked by German airborne.

1942 • All Latin American countries, except Chile and Argentina, end diplomatic relations with Germany.
- South East Asia Command set up in India.
- Operation Bolero begins.
- U.S. begins production of Liberty ships.

1943 • Admiral Karl Dönitz orders U-boats to abandon attacks in north Atlantic.
- Juan Perón rises to power in Argentina.
- Allies bomb German industry.

1944 • Red Army liberates Leningrad.
- Finland signs agreement with Soviets to end hostilities.
- U-boats use snorkel equipment.
- Brazzaville Conference held in Central Africa; Philadelphia Charter issued.
- Allies launch Big Week in Germany.
- Allies suffer high casualties at Anzio and Monte Cassino, Italy.
- Rome falls to Allies.
- Allies launch Operation Strangle.
- Operation Overlord set for D-Day: June 6, 1944.

- Allies batter their way through Normandy and drive across France.
- Allied bombing offensive against Germany increases after D-Day.
- Paris liberated.
- Hitler survives assassination in Operation Valkyrie.
- U-boats abandon French bases.
- Red Army enters Baltic States and Poland.
- Operation Market Garden fails.
- Allies launch Operation Dragoon.
- Polish Home Army revolt in Warsaw Uprising.
- RAF sinks the battleship *Tirpitz*.
- Battle of the Bulge is disastrous for Hitler.
- U.S. and RAF 2nd TAF launch largest air strike in the Ardennes.

1945 • Allies advance to Rhine River.
- Type XXIII electro-U-boats enter service and prove to be dangerous to Allies, but too little, too late.
- Germans launch Operation Baseplate air attack in Belgium, Holland, and France.
- Mussolini shot by Italian partisans.
- Allies cross the Rhine in Operation Plunder and Operation Varsity.
- General Eisenhower opts for broad sweep through Germany.
- General Bradley encircles the Ruhr.
- Allied troops liberate concentration camps; discover the horrors.
- Hitler commits suicide, April 30.
- Berlin surrenders.
- Dönitz surrenders U-boats and all naval forces.
- European war ends May 7; hostilities cease May 8.

Bibliography

Ambrose, Stephen E. *Band of Brothers: E Company, 506th Regiment, 101st Airborne from Normandy to Hitler's Eagle Nest.* New York: Simon and Schuster, 2001.

———. *Pegasus Bridge: June 6, 1944.* New York: Simon and Schuster, 1998.

Andrade, Dale. *Luzon: The United States Army Campaigns of World War II.* Washington, D.C.: Government Printing Office, 1996.

Beevor, Antony. *The Fall of Berlin, 1945.* New York: Viking Penguin, 2002.

Beschloss, Michael R. *Roosevelt, Truman, and the Destruction of Hitler's Germany, 1941–1945.* New York: Simon and Schuster, 2002.

Clay Jr., Blair. *Hitler's U-Boat War: The Hunted, 1942–1945.* New York: Random House, 1998.

D'Este, Carlo. *Eisenhower.* New York: Owl Books (Henry Holt), 2003.

Gawne, Jonathan. *Spearheading D-Day: American Special Units, 6 June 1944.* New York: Casemate Publishers, 1988.

Gilbert, Martin. *Israel: A History.* New York: William Morrow, 2002.

———. *The Righteous.* New York: Henry Holt, 2003.

———. *Second World War: A Complete History.* New York: Henry Holt, 1989.

Hapgood, David. *Monte Cassino: The Story of the Most Controversial Battle of World War II.* New York: Da Capo Press, 2002.

Irwin, John P. *Another River, Another Town: A Teenage Tank Gunner Comes of Age in Combat, 1945.* New York: Random House, 2002.

Keegan, John. *The Second World War.* New York: Penguin Books, 1990.

———. *Six Armies in Normandy: From D-Day to the Liberation of Paris.* New York: Viking Penguin, 1994.

Kimball, Warren F. *Forged in War: Roosevelt, Churchill, and the Second World War.* New York: Ivan R. Dee, Inc., 2003.

Liddell Hart, Basil. *A History of the Second World War.* New York: DaCapo Press, 1999.

Manchester, William. *American Caesar: Douglas MacArthur 1880–1963.* New York: Laureleaf, 1996.

Mann, Chris, and Christer Jorgensen. *Arctic War.* New York: St. Martin's Press, 2003.

Morison, Samuel Eliot. *Operations in North African Waters: October 1942-June 1943.* New York: Book Sales, Inc., 2001.

Murray, Williamson. *Luftwaffe, 1933–45.* Dulles, Virginia: Brasseys, 1996.

Price, Alfred. *The Last Year of the Luftwaffe: May 1944 to May 1945.* London: Greenhill Books/ Lionel Leventhal Limited, 2001.

Ryan, Cornelius. *A Bridge Too Far: The Classic History of the Greatest Airborne Battle of World War II.* New York: Simon and Schuster, 1995.

———. *Last Battle: The Classic History of the Battle for Berlin.* New York: Simon and Schuster, 1995.

Trye, Rex. *Mussolini's Soldiers.* St Paul, Minnesota: Motorbooks International, 1995.

Woodman, Richard. *Arctic Convoys 1941–1945.* London: John Murray Publications Ltd.,1996.

Zamperini, Louis: *Devil at My Heels: A WW II Hero's Epic Saga of Torment, Survival, and Forgiveness.* New York: William Morrow, 2003.

Further Information

BOOKS

Elish, Dan. *Franklin Delano Roosevelt* (Presidents and Their Times). New York: Marshall Cavendish, 2009.

Jensen, Richard, and Tim McNeese, eds. *World War II 1939-1945* (Discovering U.S. History). New York: Chelsea House, 2010.

Mara, Wil. *Kristallnacht: Nazi Persecution of the Jews in Europe* (Perspectives On). New York: Marshall Cavendish, 2010.

O'Neill, Robert, ed. *World War II: Northwest Europe 1944-1945* (Essential Histories). New York: Rosen, 2010.

WEBSITES

www.wwiimemorial.com
The U.S. National World War II Memorial.

www.hitler.org
The Hitler Historical Museum is a nonpolitical, educational resource for the study of Hitler and Nazism.

http://gi.grolier.com/wwii/wwii_ mainpage.html
The story of World War II, with biographies, articles, photographs, and films.

www.ibiblio.org/pha
Original documents on all aspects of the war.

DVDS

Great Fighting Machines of World War II. Arts Magic, 2007.

The War: A Film by Ken Burns and Lynn Novick. PBS Home Video, 2007.

World War II 360°. A & E Television Networks, 2009.

Index

NOTE: Page numbers in **bold** refer to photographs or illustrations.